CONFESSION
ALL

CONFESSION
ALL

A Humiliating, Tormented
Pilgrimage to God's Will

EDDIE TRASK

DISCLAIMER: The following body of work has been written as non-fiction. The events portrayed are expressed to the best of my knowledge and recollection. It can be asserted that all of the stories included in this book are real. However, some names and identifying traits have been rendered vague to protect the privacy of the people involved in this narrative.

Confession All © copyright 2020 by Eddie Trask. All rights reserved. No part of this book may be reproduced in any form whatsoever, by photography or xerography or by any other means, by broadcast or transmission, by translation into any kind of language, nor by recording electronically or otherwise, without permission in writing from the author, except by a reviewer, who may quote brief passages in critical articles or reviews.

ISBNs: 978-1-7352685-0-7 (pbk); 978-1-7352685-1-4 (kindle)

Front cover illustration courtesy of Riley Stark (stock photo w/ custom addition)
Cover and book design by Mayfly Design

Library of Congress Control Number: 2020916504
First Printing: 2020
Printed in the United States of America

TO ASHLEY – my gift from God

CONTENTS

Preface ix

1. Revulsion 1
2. Eyes Closed 9
3. Epiphany: Works of the Flesh 27
4. Death to Self: Calamity 51
5. Epiphany: A Log in the Eye 79
6. Death to Self: Captivity 91
7. Epiphany: As Christ Loved the Church 111
8. Death to Self: Autoimmunity 121
9. Epiphany: Sufficient Grace 135
10. Death to Self: Insanity 143
11. Eyes Open 165
12. Reflection 185

    Chronology 203
    Sources 205

Take no part in the unfruitful works of darkness, but instead expose them. For it is a shame even to speak of the things that they do in secret; but when anything is exposed by the light it becomes visible, for anything that becomes visible is light. Therefore it is said, "Awake, O sleeper, and arise from the dead, and Christ shall give you light." Look carefully then how you walk, not as unwise men but as wise, making the most of the time, because the days are evil. Therefore do not be foolish, but understand what the will of the Lord is.

PREFACE

Next to the journey itself, compiling *Confession All* was the most difficult project I've ever tackled—a sentiment which my wife, Ashley, shares. Somehow, however, in spite of all the pain and heartache, she became my best friend, helper, and editor. The fact that she was willing to go back in time and revisit every last confession, enemy attack, trigger, and thorn is extraordinary.

We agree there is only one reason to persevere through such torment: the pursuit of God and His Kingdom.

After passing through such an unconventional trial of scrupulosity, spiritual warfare, and discerning God's will, it is only fitting that I confess to you, too. You might as well know *all* of me. The old me. The confused me. The dysfunctional me. The façade me. The exposed me. And the new me.

Despite the apparent unhealthiness of it all, I was constantly convicted of which routes I was supposed to follow or avoid, regardless of how careless or idiotic it seemed. I simply know, to the best of my ability, that God permitted the following story to play out. I believe He allowed me to plumb such depths in order to comprehend the intricacies of men, women, marriage, and the Protestant Reformation. However, only He knows the true purpose.

I do not desire to have husbands follow my lead and vomit

on their spouses every sin they've ever committed. I only desire to share my story and hopefully have bits and pieces resonate with others. What anyone chooses to do with it is between them and the Holy Spirit.

No doubt, writing this book was at times cathartic, but it often served as an additional challenge, forcing me to constantly stare at and critique my weaknesses. As a result of my introspection, journaled thoughts, and attempts at writing a candid narrative without embellishment, the book itself is probably too meticulous for some readers. It is raw. It is as real as I can tell it. And in all its disordered and self-absorbed glory, it was my life.

The amount of detail is reflective of the mental torture Ashley and I endured during my scrupulous metamorphosis. Consequently, I will not run from it or conceal it. Instead, I feel called to cast light on it, while inviting others to inspect me and my motives with a magnifying glass.

The often hazy and ludicrous journey is nauseating, and may be emotionally overwhelming for some, but if you stick with me, I assure you there is hope, clarity, and redemption on the other side.

The narrative is quite non-linear and episodic, appropriately mirroring my brain during such a journey. If you get lost along the way, I've included a chronology.

As you dig into this book, here's a simple reminder: do not try this at home.

My prayers are with all who choose to proceed.

In Christ,
Eddie

1. REVULSION

Tuesday, September 5, 2017. 8:15 a.m.

"You will confess to your wife," the Holy Spirit commanded, commencing hell on earth.

It was a typical late-summer morning at Alston Park. Dozens of birds chirped, while curious dogs explored off-leash, Cabernet grapes sunbathed on lush hillsides, and hot air balloons playfully rose and descended. To Napa Valley tourists and natives, this was heaven. A disruption to such tranquility would be criminal.

Once "confess" struck my spirit, I felt a few feet shy of an aneurysm. The rhythm of my walk, often set by prayer, died. My thoughts ceased. My legs awkwardly shuffled. I knew this was not a howl of a guilt-ridden conscience. Neither angels nor demons were perched on my shoulders, taking turns whispering in my ears. The encounter was beyond comprehension. I could not escape the totality of my life, brought to the present moment as a cacophony of halts. *What just happened?* I asked myself. *That was weird.*

The sins committed since my teenage years were inaccessible. They were buried so deep—under strata of shame and denial—even my grave would've been fooled. No human knew the real Eddie—myself included.

I tried shaking the takeover, insisting it wasn't real and I had lost my mind. However, He was persistent.

I fell catatonic for a moment, then reasoned, *Maybe I can walk this off. Look—a tree...a fence...a field mouse—those should distract me. Nope—didn't work. This has to be a joke.*

Then came the first of many visceral responses: *No. This isn't real. It isn't!*

I quickly shifted to a longer hiking path, giving myself time to reason with God and my psyche. I desperately prayed, *Dear Father...* Dead end! Then I sang, *Worthy is the Lamb...* Dead end! Every attempt to seek asylum was greeted with static. I was surrounded by beauty, yet set ablaze, frantically looking to be extinguished. Such a dichotomy would soon become typical. Within thirty minutes—as my chin inched closer to my sternum—I had exhausted all measures.

Approaching my car, reality crushed me. *This is real*, I lamented. *I can't escape this. I'll confess, come what may.*

While driving home, I decided an assault of ice picks to Ashley's heart was best suited for the weekend. *I'm being considerate*, I thought. Upon arriving, I acted "myself." Ashley looked up from reading a book to Arlo and Eviana, four and one, respectively.

"How was the walk, sweetie?" she asked. She was often endearing in tone; an effort now heightened since the recent loss of my job.

With a normal fake face, I responded, "Good," then whisked out of the room.

A quick change of clothes, an email refresh, and a trip to the toilet paved my first detour. I then bought time in the kitchen, grabbing raisins, a banana, and a bottle of water. Now off to errands. *I'll figure out where I need to go once I'm in the car*, I thought. My façade was evaporating with no sanctuary in sight. My popular coping mechanisms and escape chutes were about to become obsolete. I had to stay busy.

1. Revulsion

As the day progressed, the risk and burden of confession multiplied. To suspend Ashley's sorrow and my responsibility, I attempted punting a football of courage down a field of cowardice. And because I suddenly remembered a Friday job interview and poker night, my excuses for delay were legitimate. Knowing cardiac arrest was imminent, who wouldn't stall for a few days?

■ ■ ■

Very little seemed genuine or Biblical our first eight years of marriage. Often accusatory, argumentative, and complacent, we were anesthetized roommates. Our closest moments were in front of the television, at restaurants, or while enjoying wine and cheese on the couch. In and of themselves, they were not harmful; however, they represented a critical issue: perceived bonding—truthfully, sedated survival—occurred when a third "person" was involved. TV, wine, and food were kickstands. We couldn't just sit and talk. Reality was a far cry from our ideals, exponentially detaching us and making us increasingly wrong to the other.

Ashley did not feel love from me, and I did not feel respect from her—and funnily enough, both of us would've claimed we were trying to meet each other's needs in our own way, driven by our own understanding of how a spouse should be treated.

We knew we needed help. Something enormous was missing. We spoke of therapy several times. We even went once, then bailed after two meetings. I wanted to keep going; she didn't, lest she be reminded of her failures. I had exposed and repeatedly reminded her of her faults, and because mine were hidden (well, at least the most shameful things), she felt she was the cause of most—if not all—of our dysfunction. She didn't want the weight piled higher—especially not in front of me. She was already slogging.

So, we individually saw therapists. Ashley was vulnerably

highlighting her mistakes with her counselor, while I was down the road highlighting her mistakes with my counselor. I chose to hide "among the trees of the garden" (Genesis 3:8). I had to.

Of course, our family pictures were filled with rehearsed smiles, hiding unhappiness and emptiness. Year after year after year. After a while, we weren't acting. We had become new characters. We had to.

Act normal, and no one will sense a thing.

■ ■ ■

Ashley was raised religiously conservative. Because of her moral convictions, introversion, and timidity, she was often labeled a goody-goody. As a teenager, her parents' divorce amplified these traits. Depression and fear of abandonment were then added to the mix. And due to a thyroid condition she developed at the age of eight, extreme fatigue kept her sidelined for years. It all led to blurry memories and numbness.

Her best attributes were off my radar. Instead, I saw that she was insecure and subtly resistant. She was not hidden like me, but distanced. Regardless, I knew her very well. Her "confession" had been on display since we met. I knew the real her. She was Ashley; I wasn't Eddie. If she sensed a problem, her opinion was voiced immediately. I painted her constantly dissatisfied. If I sensed a problem, I held on to it until resentment formed a geyser. I'm sure this painted me secretly, constantly dissatisfied with instability thrown in. She hit smothering singles; I hit firestorm homers.

We met at a Starbucks when a barista gave Ashley's drink to me by mistake. I was struck by her smile when I told her about the mishap, then proceeded to stay and wait for her friend to leave her side so I could introduce myself. An hour later, as the store closed, we were all asked to leave. I scrambled in my car for something to write on. Frantically, seeing her friend was still

1. Revulsion

welded to her as they neared the parking lot, I wrote my name and number on a landscaper's business card, ran to give it to her, said an awkward "Here you go", then turned away and tripped on the curb.

"I'm Ashley, by the way," she said as I headed back to my car. Over my shoulder, I responded, "Oh...I'm Eddie. Nice to meet you."

Less than twenty-four hours later, we met at an Italian restaurant. As we sat outside, taking turns sharing our likes and dislikes, sunlight streamed through some patio plants and illuminated the side of her face. *What an angel*, I thought.

I could not believe she would go on a date with me. Admittedly, however, I was the "nicest" guy a girl could meet, so why was I surprised?

■ ■ ■

Twelve hours after the Alston Park confrontation, Arlo and Eviana were in bed. Ashley and I grabbed glasses of water and settled on the couch. Usually, a few words were muttered on opposite ends of our seven-seater couch, followed by ten to twenty minutes on social media, then a strategic approach to our queue of TV shows. This typically got us to 10:30 or 11 p.m., then it was off to bed.

Ashley looked at me with a half-smile. I was sure she would sense my fear. I had mentally exited the house, driven out of town, and was looking for a new costume—but all backup plans were gone. The single bulb in our corner lamp had never been so aggravating. The perfect setting to cement such a horrific memory: the sun had nodded off; only darkness filled the hall, den, and kitchen; and the television acted as a large mirror. Adrenaline unmasked my guilty face. *The time is now.*

Hesitantly, Ashley asked, "What's wrong?"

"I...I have something to tell you. I don't really know how to say it." Her body tensed. "There was something I didn't mention in the baptismal tank. Something I've been dealing with for decades...."

I stared at a loose thread in our rug. Ashley was frozen.

My head slowly lifted. "Pornography. I've been viewing pornography." *At least I didn't cheat in-person,* I told myself.

She sat paralyzed. "What?"

"I've been dealing with this since I was a teenager," I said. It felt like minutes passed, then I began answering sensible—but humiliating—questions. "Yes—throughout marriage. Yes—during engagement. Yes—in our favorite hotels. Yes—throughout the house. Yes—while we dated. Yes—just assume the answer is yes," I conceded.

Within minutes, twenty-plus years of shame were spread out in disorderly fashion on our coffee table, or so I thought. *This is good, right? I'm obedient.*

We each caught our breath. As I slumped in the most nauseated state I've known, Ashley did the same.

Then, "Why? How frequent?"

Even though it seemed counterproductive, it was time. Cats were pouring out of the bag, never to return.

"Oh—I guess there were times after baptism, too," I whispered.

"You just said it had ended by then," Ashley responded. "You lied?"

As the evening continued, my speech and heart rate were diametrically opposed. Ashley's eyes would meet mine every few minutes, then immediately divert to a wall. She was oddly composed. Then came another confession. Without warning, she stood up in horror and bolted out of the room, heading straight for the garage. She was a volcano—yet considerate of the kids sleeping down the hall. The night ended with her releasing two bloodcurdling screams.

1. Revulsion

Still on the couch, I could not sink any lower. With her cries contending with cement slabs and 1962 insulation, I expected police to pound on the door within minutes.

■ ■ ■

For the next three days, sin recollections alternated between light streams and deluges. I answered a river of questions, at first believing *pornography* to be a catch-all. Certainly, God wanted this one thing revealed, but now I could rest. Then, like blunt force to the head, I realized, *This is only one part of one layer*. Pornography was a mere slice in my pie of falsehood.

"Ash, there's more," I admitted.

With a lifeless stare, she said nothing.

Even with extreme resistance, my wheels were turning. I rushed to turn off my memory faucet, only to have its handle snap off in my hand.

Here goes nothing–and everything, I thought.

"Well, yeah, I ended up at a strip club. I was drunk and wandering around. I hadn't planned it." *At least we weren't married at the time.* "Yes—there were lap dances. Yes—she allowed me to touch her." *At least I didn't have sex.*

Ashley shut down. No words, just a wrenched heart on display. My pre- and during-marriage confessions were now married, forming a snapshot of my life and a pattern of confessions to come.

"I called a stripper to come to my room but bailed at the last minute." *At least I cancelled.*

"I was drunk. I was only at the club for ten minutes. I couldn't handle it." *I'm a good guy. She doesn't get it.*

...But why does it hurt so much to confess?

"How could I have been so naïve?" Ashley sobbed.

My act had been so advanced, I had forgotten I was playing

a character; I was officially conjoined—with look-at-the-bright-side excuses always in the chamber.

For years, I must have been asking, *How can I expertly balance secret rebellion and visible compliance?* Whether I committed the act or not was suddenly irrelevant. I finally caught a glimpse of my reprehensible cravings through the lens of another. Yet, I still entertained pitiful thoughts: *I shouldn't have done that, but it was all justified.*

I wanted to blame it all on Ashley. All of it. However, my parasitic immorality long preceded her. You see, I brought no carry-ons on our marriage flight—only checked baggage.

Ashley had never known the extent of my depravity.

Until I opened my mouth, neither had I.

There I sat in residual filth, knowing I had never been a disciple of Jesus Christ—only a confused, arrogant, nice-enough impostor who had purchased a one-way ticket to hell, believing it said heaven.

2. EYES CLOSED

But we must not suppose that even if we succeeded in making everyone nice we should have saved their souls. A world of nice people, content in their own niceness, looking no further, turned away from God, would be just as desperately in need of salvation as a miserable world—and might even be more difficult to save.

—C. S. Lewis

I achieved a lot externally. I attended church workshops, was baptized, and responded to altar calls. I tried. Boy, did I try. Or, at least, my biased memory tells me I tried. Frighteningly, these efforts birthed false hope.

For years I occasionally read the Bible, often writing favorite verses in notebooks—from pride to sexuality, the highlighted themes were personal to me, but I didn't adopt their messages. Reading led to hundreds of eyes-squinted nods, as if to say, "That's good. That's really good." Although gaining head knowledge, I resisted submission, capturing the surface only; nothing pierced my ego's membrane. But at least I was kind. If people were to ask, "Is Eddie a nice guy?", overwhelmingly, "Yes" was the answer. Being nice is the summit of Christian morality, right?

How did I become nice? I stood for nothing and everything at once. I was so nice (and weak), I would have watched someone drive off a collapsed bridge before warning of danger. I was a non-confrontational chameleon who refused to oppose most viewpoints, lest I be judged. *I'd rather be a coward*, I'm sure I thought subconsciously. Plus, how could I stand with Christ's teachings while soaking in grave—though buried—sins? So, my opinion morphed according to the crowd, regardless of the topic. Unless drunk, I was deathly afraid to commit to any clear position. This way everyone would like me. My fear-of-man disguise: a neutered, neutral party. This also meant no one would have access to my vault. Nevertheless, a nice person doesn't really sin, right?

And if I didn't really sin to begin with, why would I need God as my authority? I wouldn't have to lose my life, take up my cross, and forfeit my wayward tendencies.

Deep down, I knew I was a sinner, but an ocean lies between merely perceiving sin and abhorring it.

Smells & Bells

I was seven when I first served on the altar. Living by an expanded-upon Vince Lombardi rule, if we arrived at Mass ten minutes early, we were twenty minutes late. My mom instilled punctuality; my dad instilled work ethic. With plenty of time to spare, my brother David and I stood around, dressed in our finely pressed cassocks, talking about God knows what.

Mass was multi-sensory, to say the least. I vividly remember closing my eyes, bowing my head, and folding my hands. Incense wafted around me as I moved my hand from side to side to watch smoke curl around my fingers; candles flickered when I

2. Eyes Closed

finally got them to light (burrowing under wax, their wicks were like ingrown hairs); pew creaks and toddler squeals filled the echo-chamber sanctuary; and ringing bells silenced whispers.

I recall an ornate screen, no more than 8 x 10-inches, partitioning the sacristy and sanctuary that resembled a balsa wood lattice—so thin and tempting. David and I often joked about the urge to punch a hole through it. We had taken a few karate classes from an instructor who lived in a van. I think he inspired us. He taught us how to "bop" a dog on the head if it attacked. Money well spent.

David sat across the altar from me, always next to the priest. As the more proper, disciplined, and distinguished one, he didn't fidget like I did. He was a robot, while I had restless legs. I admired him. Intimidated by his duties, I couldn't imagine having to take his place if he got sick. I was the guy who mostly needed to sit, kneel, and look patient. I felt like a fixture, barely capable of placing the processional crucifix in its newly welded stand. A talented parishioner's gift to the parish. One of the things I loved about the small town of Kerman.

On many Sundays, I recall quiet footsteps approaching us at 9:55 a.m.—always a parishioner asking if we could cover for the classic no-call, no-show altar servers. With obligation, I frustratedly—yet pridefully—walked to the sacristy to get dressed. I'm sure David thought nothing of it.

Over the years, I served on the altar with three different priests. Despite popular, preconceived notions of the Catholic priesthood, each Father was kind and pious. However, because jokes were all too common, I had to defend my altar boy beginnings, insisting sexual abuse and altar serving are not mutually inclusive. After a while, I only mentioned my background in Catholic circles, which became increasingly rare in my twenties, and non-existent into my thirties.

Through my nearly ten years of serving, I went in and out

of devotion, in and out of caring, and in and out of understanding. I was confused about what I was doing, why I was doing it, and where any of it was referenced in the Bible (as if I would've researched). Even with years of Catechism, I was a novice who struggled to submit to an ultimate authority, often choosing pride as my leader. Yet, I could go through the motions like nobody's business, even while asking, *Why do I have to do so much?*

I have to wonder if I foolishly concluded, *If I don't fully listen, I won't be fully responsible.* I now know that's called vincible ignorance.

Upon graduating high school, I was yards from the Catholic Church. By the end of college, I was miles.

Calls & Falls

Six years later, with all eyes closed and heads bowed—now attending a Protestant, non-denominational church—the pastor lifted his voice to the congregation and said, "...If that's you, if you're distant from God, if you want to get right with Him and you're feeling a tug on your heart, raise your hand and look up at me."

My hand lifted with a resistance band of shame, taking a few seconds to complete the motion. But I did it. I made eye contact, too.

One after another, the pastor acknowledged those who had committed to the Lord. "The gentleman in the back, yes, praise God. The lady in the red shirt, I see you. The group of guys in the center here. Yes!"

Within a few minutes, after a raucous applause and a brief explanation of what it means to be saved, he continued, "Now, if you raised your hand, I'd ask that you come to the front for prayer."

Moments later, I wept near the stage. Kleenexes in hand, I

2. Eyes Closed 13

mumbled gibberish to an associate pastor. I didn't know why I was crying. Peripherally, I saw dozens of others. Validation.

A few years later, I lifted my hand to recommit my life to the Lord, realizing my initial altar call response didn't alter me—never mind the many times I felt prompted to respond, only to back out, insisting it wasn't the Holy Spirit who had called. Through these years I embraced my own strength, weakening each time. Whenever I felt regret, it was superficial and always accompanied by an *I'll repent tomorrow* attitude. As stated in 2 Corinthians 7:10, "For godly grief produces a repentance that leads to salvation and brings no regret, but worldly grief produces death." When moved to tears, it wasn't about a desire for dramatic change, but simply due to something missing.

Still, I wasn't sure what caused my public recommitment. Using my marketer's brain, I speculated, *Was it the quantity of "impressions" that finally led to "conversion"? Was I genuinely wanting change, or was I weak at that moment? Did I feel air conditioning on the back of my neck, or was that the Holy Spirit? No—that's crazy. I was sitting near the vents, though.*

I was rolling in dirt, getting up, and dusting myself off—only to return to dirt. "Like a dog that returns to his vomit is a fool that repeats his folly" (Proverbs 26:11). This was life. Sin, remorse, occasional repentance (always half-hearted, it seemed), sin, sin, sin, guilt, sin, some remorse, justification of sin, more sin, sin, sin, deep remorse, worldly grief, shame, justification of sin, sin, sin—I could go on like this the rest of the book, never capturing the hopelessness of such an exhausting, demoralizing cycle.

In the middle of these patterns, I often recited my past, reinforcing excuses. Traumas played in my head, usually in petrifying detail. These either led to justified anger, shame, guilt, or continual grieving—all acting as bait-stick snares. It was always about how these episodes impacted *me*, not others.

As I fought to resist sin, I recalled these memories, then sank in self-pity and succumbed to temptation. After I mustered willpower and climbed out of a ditch, I then strangely fought to justify the next sin. This not only dropped me back to the bottom, but erased the joy of progress, which made future efforts more challenging and seemingly pointless.

I was now less likely to wrestle with pros and cons and, instead, simply immerse myself in selfishness.

I recall wanting to drink another glass of wine while at an event years earlier. *You should stop*, I told myself. *It's only 8 p.m.* Then, as only one affected by poor judgment can do, I refused my brain a chance to argue further. I was halfway through the next glass when I remembered what I had told myself ten minutes earlier. By then, my judgment's line in the sand had moved considerably. By the next glass, the line was gone. And who was responsible for such a disaster? It had to have been Ashley or some repressed victim card. Regardless, in my mind, all options justified my behavior.

But even if I had "seared my conscience with an iron," I was guilty. Resisting the Holy Spirit (or turning off my internal gauge) did not make me innocent; it made me an ignorant child, arrogant enough to think I could game my fate.

Altar calls provided temporary life support, dragging me to the shallow end of the pool. I'd catch a breath, overconfidently play a game of Marco Polo, grab an ice cream sandwich, then plunge into the deep end again.

And again.

And again.

Whitewashed Tomb

It's strange to use the plural of baptism. The only instance of rebaptism is found in Acts 19:1-7:

2. Eyes Closed

> While Apol'los was at Corinth, Paul passed through the upper country and came to Ephesus. There he found some disciples. And he said to them, "Did you receive the Holy Spirit when you believed?" And they said, "No, we have never even heard that there is a Holy Spirit." And he said, "Into what then were you baptized?" They said, "Into John's baptism." And Paul said, "John baptized with the baptism of repentance, telling the people to believe in the one who was to come after him, that is, Jesus." On hearing this, they were baptized in the name of the Lord Jesus.

Yet, "rebaptisms" occur every weekend at churches around the world: immersion, decades after a sprinkling or pouring.

As an infant, I certainly couldn't comprehend such an action; as an adult, however...I still didn't comprehend.

I was blind to the fact that there is one baptism for the forgiveness of sins, and the context of Acts 19 is quite different than a modern-day debate about infant vs. adult baptism.

Before making my decision, I recall several strong convictions while watching others profess their faith in Christ. I first ignored such a conviction in November 2016, internally yelling, *I have already been baptized!* Several months passed before I finally emailed the church staff to inquire about the process, confident the Holy Spirit was leading. At this point, I was unsure of what baptism meant but surely felt it would bring me closer to heaven because this time it was *my* choice. I then jumbled my own definition together: one part symbolic, one part salvific, one part grace, one part faith, one part burial, one part repentance, one part born again, and one part freedom. As a confused church attendee, I'm sure somewhere I wondered, *Do I even want to understand what it means?*

Was I chasing a silver bullet?

On the evening of February 25, 2017, I stood in a baptismal

tank sharing a premature, fractional testimony. It felt liberating to share my story, but complete transparency was not an option; instead, I decided to use alcohol abuse as the focal point. I reasoned, *It isn't as taboo as pornography, right? Certainly, drunkenness is a big-ticket sin, isn't it? It's on par with pornography, right? If I cast light on alcohol, that satisfies honesty, doesn't it? Releasing some shame is better than none. Who says my testimony needs to include all my sins anyway? Actually, do I need to say anything? God will understand. This explicit, public announcement (or renouncement) of sins isn't even in the Bible, is it?*

Public testimony aside, I committed to never discuss sexual immorality with *anyone*, regardless of who they were. Shame sought to remain the undisputed, undefeated heavyweight champion of my world. In the tank, the heaviest I had ever been, I proved to be a worthy weight-class opponent. *I hope this changes me*, I thought.

The following months were good indeed. I lost weight and gained confidence; I didn't drink and I lied less; I listened to worship music; prayed more often; and glanced at Bible verses occasionally. The outside of my cup was much cleaner.

> Woe to you, scribes and Pharisees, hypocrites! for you cleanse the outside of the cup and of the plate, but inside they are full of extortion and rapacity. You blind Pharisee! first cleanse the inside of the cup and of the plate, that the outside also may be clean. Woe to you, scribes and Pharisees, hypocrites! for you are like whitewashed tombs, which outwardly appear beautiful, but within they are full of dead men's bones and all uncleanness. So you also

2. Eyes Closed 17

> outwardly appear righteous to men, but within you are full of hypocrisy and iniquity.
>
> —Matthew 23:25-28

However, a closer look revealed my weight loss was directly tied to an urgent lifestyle and diet change (which included strict avoidance of alcohol) driven by a longing to rectify digestive issues I had been fighting for a decade. Proudly, I thought outsiders would say, "Hey, baptism really does work. Look at Eddie. He's looking better already." Acting in my own strength, I applied checklists to deter sin, and used artificial criteria to elevate myself. Pride in one of its lowest forms, I'm convinced.

> Fine feelings, new insights, greater interest in "religion" mean nothing unless they make our actual behavior better; just as in an illness "feeling better" is not much good if the thermometer shows that your temperature is still going up. In that sense the outer world is quite right to judge Christianity by its results. Christ told us to judge by results. [...] When we Christians behave badly, or fail to behave well, we are making Christianity unbelievable to the outside world.
>
> —C. S. Lewis

In the following months leading up to my confession to Ashley, I slowly let off the gas. A "Christian" not ready to put his hand to the plow. Afraid of manual labor, I suppose.

At a business meeting with an old friend, I had a couple of glasses of wine (*I don't want to be rude to him. Plus, it's his treat*).

Leading up to an out-of-town event, I had a drink in my hand at the airport, on the plane, and at lunch when I landed. It felt obligatory. *I have denied myself all these months. A few drinks won't mess up my diet progress.* By the end of the day, however, I was almost blackout drunk.

For poker night, I brought a six-pack of gluten-free beer. *I'll have two, then give the rest away.* A few hours in, however, I was down to one bottle, having quickly drunk the others, not wanting to share with anyone. I was acting like a ravenous competitor the way I had with my brother. Even with cereal, pizza, and ice cream, we competed to essentially "get in the last word"—be that the last bowl, slice, or scoop. Then it struck me: *Why would any of these guys choose a gluten-free beer over wine, whiskey, or Sierra Nevada?* By then, though, it didn't matter. I was drunk again, now caravanning to In-N-Out at midnight. Only two weeks before confession.

While intoxicated, even mildly buzzed, pornography was a given, which I could've sworn I'd drowned in baptism.

As irreverent as it sounds, I had exhausted altar calls and baptisms and remained a slave to sin. *Were they in and of themselves saviors? Were they guaranteeing a change of heart? Were they supposed to force surrender and obedience?*

Traumaddict

Even with grace at work within me, internal wounds continually overruled it. I was a security guard at my own sporting event, asking God to show His ticket. Once I saw it was labeled "repent and live" and not "more excuses," I wanted nothing to do with it. I needed to maintain backup plans and escape hatches. My excuses' vital signs were of dire importance.

For the length of my marriage, and for many years preceding it, I was comforted by reliving terrible memories and reciting pain. At the time, I didn't know why. It seemed abnormal, but I couldn't—or wouldn't—stop. Once a few memories were in the queue, their weight carried to subsequent traumas—whether I

2. Eyes Closed

had a job or not, Ashley and I were closely connected or not, or I felt respected or not. And when I wasn't recreating specific events, I amassed rejections, offenses, and pities like they were diversification tools. They resulted in dozens of replaying spirals, always leading to sinful conclusions. My hippocampus housed a behemoth snowball of *Eddie's lowlights* racing down a black-diamond run, absorbing everything in its path: trees, animals, a ski lodge. I ensured the links between trauma, unforgiveness, and sin were indestructible. Truly, a victim's paradise.

For years—as challenges arose at work, home, or on the road—predictable, well-worn thoughts circled: *She doesn't like me; I'm constantly rejected; Why does everything happen to me?; What horrible luck I have; Why?; Why?; Why?!; I'll do whatever I want; $%&#!; I'm justified.*

■ ■ ■

In December 2002, five years before I met Ashley, I was a seventh wheel at a rock concert in San Jose. As the night progressed in the rafters of a massive venue, I coped with loneliness by ordering a series of drinks. Using a friend's ID, I acted as if the alcohol content in beer (truthfully, Mike's Hard Lemonade) was that of water. By the end of the concert, I was barely standing.

Back at my friend's house, everyone with gas left in the tank was on the patio smoking and drinking. I reclined in the living room, daydreaming about how to get home, even though someone had insisted I spend the night. After thirty minutes, I concluded: *You're good.* With severely diluted judgment, I grabbed my keys and maneuvered to my car like an Inflatable Tube Man.

Nearly twenty minutes into the drive, nearly blackout drunk, I realized I was on the wrong freeway. Miraculously, I got off at the next exit.

As I climbed a slight grade, I didn't slow. At forty-five mph, I bypassed a stop sign and slammed into a guardrail. I was a trashed test dummy, with my Accord now an Accord-ion (a pathetic joke I told to lessen severity). I came to, found a truck driver down the road who witnessed the whole thing, paid him twenty dollars to get me to Palo Alto, then convinced my uncle, Bill (UB, as we called him), to drive me back to the scene an hour later to assess the damage. After 1 a.m., we approached the officer-heavy accident scene. I handed myself over, explaining the hit-and-run.

"How many drinks have you had?" the officer asked.

"Two or three," I lied.

"What were you doing tonight?"

"I went to a concert with some friends, ate a burrito, then drove home," I responded.

I failed every field sobriety test. In handcuffs, I motioned goodbye to UB. As we headed to the hospital, I apologized to the officers for all the trouble. I'm sure I thanked myself for showing respect. Prideful even then. *Still not a broken bone,* I said to myself.

"You reek of alcohol. I hope you learned something," the nurse said, motherly in her concern. "Honestly, what were you thinking?"

I spent the night in the Santa Rita Jail drunk tank among dozens who spent half the night trying to one-up each other's misdemeanor and felony stories. Meanwhile, the communal, barrier-less toilet got its share of use. Breakfast was an orange and the last bologna sandwich I ever ate.

■ ■ ■

A DUI accident should have taught me to stay on the straight and narrow, but it only worked until my uncle committed suicide a few years later.

I received a call at work from Ted, UB's lifelong friend and

2. Eyes Closed

coworker. He was so close to our family, we considered him part of it.

"Eddie, UB didn't come to work today. We're a little worried. We haven't heard a word. Do you know anything?" he asked.

"No. I don't. Let me call GP [Grandpa]. I'll be in touch," I said.

Within a minute, I was on the phone with GP.

"He didn't take his medicine with him. He said he was going on a short trip. I'm sure we'll hear from him soon," he summarized.

Panic overcame me. *Two days without medication? Oh no.*

Within a few hours, I received another call from Ted. "We found his Pathfinder in a parking lot adjacent to a train crossing," he said. "I called the police. I'll keep you up to date."

"Okay," I said. "Thank you." I turned to my brother, who was on shift with me. We hugged and cried. We hoped for the best while wrestling off the worst.

I motioned to my boss. "We need to leave right now."

"No problem, man," he replied, watching a new set of tears well up in our eyes.

Within an hour, I got another call. "I don't know how to say this...." At that point, no matter how it was said, I had guessed what was next. "We found a note he left on the passenger seat, and his body is believed to have been found. The coroner's office will use dental records to confirm. I'm so sorry."

In shock, the whole family drove to Palo Alto to comfort GP, who had been living with my uncle for the past five years. I lived with them for two and a half of those years.

Naively, I reread UB's suicide note for well over two years. Even with counseling, I was paralyzed in grief. As with the best kind of friends, our relationship was marked by the little things:

I'll never forget catching Caltrain to Giants games. We often grabbed maple bars at the corner donut shop before entering the stadium. We witnessed at least four of Barry Bonds' Splash Hits, including number six when he handed his bat to John McEnroe—both legends in my uncle's eyes. There was nothing—absolutely nothing—more satisfying in sports than a night game at PacBell Park with kayaks crowded in McCovey Cove, hundreds of flashbulbs, and Gordon Biersch garlic fries in hand.

We also saw Bonds' season-record seventy-third home run off a Dennis Springer knuckleball. I bet it was no more than sixty-five mph. We actually saw Bonds hesitate for a split second, then connect with his classic swing—as textbook as Ken Griffey Jr.'s. My uncle snapped a picture, perfectly capturing the ball between Bonds' bat and the Old Navy sign in right field. I have no idea what happened to the picture, but it was stunning. Baseball was one of our many escapes.

It was a mallet to my temples when UB died. To deal with the resulting pain, I found a drinking companion: every subgenre of metal music. Medicine for my anger was logical at the time. I used UB's suffering to add another layer of rebar and cement to my victimhood foundation. In addition, to creatively cope, I often pictured myself with superhuman strength jumping in front of the train and stopping it dead while cars piled up behind in a zigzag.

■ ■ ■

A few years later, I was at Fresno State, carrying a folder with my just-approved graduate program application. Full of pride, I thought, *I'll have my MBA in less than two years!* I'm sure I was smiling—if not on the outside, certainly somewhere. With my car in the distance, I began to cross the main campus intersection. With a nanosecond to spare, I peripherally saw a bumper geared to strike my left leg. I went airborne. I had wings for what felt like three seconds, the way MJ must have felt when taking off a half step inside the free-throw line—except not. I had

2. Eyes Closed

rolled onto a hood and slammed into a windshield. Then a sudden brake detoured my motion, which ended with a pavement bounce. I knew none of this, of course. Only flight.

Completely lost, I got up and headed straight for my car, wanting to drive home. I figured a few bruises were fine. However, I was apparently spurting a bit.

"Dude, you're bleeding!" a student yelled.

I pressed my hand against my forehead as he took the shirt off his back and insisted on wrapping it around my head. As a guy who used to put Band-Aids on paper cuts, I hesitated to release my hand.

By then, a dozen people gathered, assuring me the paramedics were on their way. While I waited in the driver's seat of the girl who had hit me, my eyelids drooped. I recall bystanders reminding me to stay awake as I gazed through a kaleidoscope. *How did my body do this?* I probably smiled on the inside, knowing I *was* of football quality. *Why didn't my high school friends believe me? Still not a broken bone.* Prideful even then.

■ ■ ■

A few years later:

As a result of UB's death, I called GP on a very regular basis. Even if the chats were five to ten minutes long, we cherished them. One week he wasn't answering his phone. I tried on a Monday, then the following day. Nothing. There were occasional days when he was visiting with a neighbor or out at the grocery store when I called, so I didn't give it much thought. I didn't panic until I tried for the third consecutive day. This time, I told Ashley I feared the worst. She and I had been dating six months, yet I could already see in her a deep concern for my family.

"You better call your dad," she said.

Within a minute, I was lightly shaking on the phone.

"Yeah, that's odd. Why don't you head there now?" my dad asked. "I'll get dressed and leave immediately."

He was about three hours away, and I was half as close.

"Okay. In the meantime, I'll call Ted. Maybe he can knock on the door," I said.

When I was within forty-five minutes of GP's house, Ted called me back. "No answer," he said.

As I approached Palo Alto, I called the fire department stationed less than a block from the house.

We drove up at the same time. I sprinted to the front door, unlocked it, and found GP face down on the ground, barely breathing. He had fallen five days earlier and had been desperately crawling around the house trying to pull himself up, in and out of consciousness. A stalwart veteran of WWII's 801st Tank Destroyer Battalion.

Once he was released from a subacute rehabilitation center, Ashley and I visited every weekend for months. We bought groceries, watched reruns of *Gunsmoke*, and changed his foot bandages (his heels had developed necrosis and needed debridement). Oddly, these car trips were conducive to some of our best conversations.

Four years later, on GP's deathbed, Ashley whispered she was pregnant with Arlo. With eyes closed, GP lifted his right fist in approval. He knew before I did. She wanted to leave him with a special thought.

■ ■ ■

Through it all, as a twenty-six-year-old, I had witnessed the tragic, the extraordinary, and the depressing—later thinking an angel was with all of us, no matter how grim, shocking, or seemingly irredeemable the experience. But, because sin is opportunistic, each memory became a devastating monument of victimhood. Thank God I was at least nice!

2. Eyes Closed

And if these traumas had not been a part of my life, you bet I would've found others. It's pretty easy. Excuses for rebellion grow on trees.

3. EPIPHANY: WORKS OF THE FLESH

Now the works of the flesh are plain: fornication, impurity, licentiousness, idolatry, sorcery, enmity, strife, jealousy, anger, selfishness, dissension, party spirit, envy, drunkenness, carousing, and the like. I warn you, as I warned you before, that those who do such things shall not inherit the kingdom of God.

—Galatians 5:19-21

As in water face answers to face, so the mind of man reflects the man. Sheol and Abaddon are never satisfied, and never satisfied are the eyes of man.

—Proverbs 27:19-20

All things are full of weariness; a man cannot utter it; the eye is not satisfied with seeing, nor the ear filled with hearing.

—Ecclesiastes 1:8

For all that is in the world, the lust of the flesh and the lust of the eyes and the pride of life, is not of the Father but is of the

> *world. And the world passes away, and the lust of it; but he who does the will of God abides for ever.*
>
> —1 John 2:16-17

These verses are clear, yet, while in darkness, they might as well have been translated in wingdings or hieroglyphics. Sadly, I'm convinced I could have read them—even studied them at length—and remained blind. And since Holy Scripture didn't seem to deter my behavior, neither did hard statistics or vague anecdotes. However, I don't fault the playwright or the antagonist; I blame the main, counterfeit character. My hardened shell needed dynamite, not chisels, yet I feared an explosion.

I can hear Ashley over the years, highly critical and leery of popular culture, often citing its obsession with sexuality and its ever-changing barometer.

"Why is this shown in the middle of the day?" she asked during a nearly pornographic commercial. "Who is the audience? Everyone?" The inference was: *Shouldn't this garbage be reserved for darker hours? If the disgraceful must exist, can it at least wait until kids are in bed?*

I responded with a typical, "I know, huh? What a joke." Desiring to protect our kids, I was very much in agreement, confused about blatant attempts to sexualize any and everything. However, I was also the guy viewing pornography in the middle of the day. I, too, didn't save the disgraceful for darker hours. I only had to close a door and turn on a screen. Closed hinges transported me from 2 p.m. to 2 a.m.

But I couldn't see the hypocrisy. I refused to see it.

From the pulpit I could've heard, "Seventy percent of Christian men view pornography!"—or maybe the number was fifty percent, or ninety-eight percent, or ten percent. Regardless, none of these numbers—none—would have mattered to a person who believed his sins were reasonable and warranted. I could do the same with divorce, virginity, and cohabitation statistics. As with any sin data, it shocked me for a few hours, then became a blurry memory I may have loosely referenced when wanting to internally validate my struggle or when making odd, self-serving statements like, "Jesus needs to come soon," "We're in trouble," or "It's bad out there." As if I did not represent the bad.

I'm not sure if survey results caused disbelief, made me feel normal, or both. Nevertheless, with any measure of godly sorrow and humility, I would've recognized I was a member of pornography's demand, fueling an industry supplied with daughters, sisters, and mothers {Insert vomit}. Plus, as I now know, these women are often trafficked {Insert more vomit}.

And with Society's Law acting as a god, demand is an insatiable stage-4 cancer.

Nothing New Under the Sun

Strangely, supply seems to be in lockstep with demand, creating market equilibrium. Pornographic images and connotations are not just represented in videos and magazines typically synonymous with pornography. They permeate everywhere: in movies, books, songs, advertisements, grocery stores, malls, and outlets; at beaches; on leisurely walks, posters, and newsstands. From clothing and cosmetics to technology and food and beverage, branding is often centered on the female body, as if the appeal to entice purchase otherwise dies. I've seen it on boxes of cereal, cartons of ice cream, and bottles of tea. Nearly anything can stoke the flame of lust, even if under the appearance of "It's innocent!"

However, even if our current climate was the worst in history (which I now doubt; see *sacred prostitution* for comparison), I'd have no excuse. As much as I clung to my irresistible idol of moral relativism, God does not provide me leeway based on the year—be it 2020, 1370, 535, or 57 AD. But why on earth would I want to live by absolutes? Why would I desire to be subject to a supreme authority—an authority who calls for a denial of flesh?

No matter how much I desired to hear it, God would not tell me, *Oh, you lusted today, huh? Go ahead and blame the world, blame the women around you, blame anyone or anything that entices you. After all, you're not in control of your body. You have free will in every area except this one? How fitting.*

I asked myself:

- *If a primetime network airs a show on par with what was deemed pornography seventy years ago, is it less offensive to God?*
- *Does He make concessions for me or amend commands to better suit my struggles?*
- *Does lust only exist at the moment culture defines it? Actually, would culture even dare to define such a moving target?*

For years my thoughts were replaced with those of large networks. I assumed because most of the country accessed the same programming, it must be okay. I was Linus, and my blanket was groupthink. I should have fled. By watching and endorsing these shows, I grew too comfortable in the world. The line between Christian and non-Christian got fuzzier and fuzzier until it disappeared, at which point I was simply a nice person living a good life. I was immersed in the world, and yet because I proclaimed Christ, was I somehow getting a free pass?

As Romans 6:1-2 states, "What shall we say then? Are we to continue in sin that grace may abound? By no means! How can we who died to sin still live in it?"

I did not understand grace and God's static commands, unmoved by the times. I felt I could navigate and obey based

3. Epiphany: Works Of The Flesh

on the world's moral compass. Even the "believing" world was shouting at me, *God is love!*, which—while true—easily became, *Therefore you really are a good person*. However, something wasn't adding up: If I have free will, and I believe in objective rights and wrongs, is it possible to win the race regardless of the choices I make? A jailbreak hack, if you will. Do I not flirt with momentary *and* eternal consequences for my behavior? I give my children consequences, but am I to teach that what I ask of them will become irrelevant as they discover *God is love*? Would this lead to a just God? Do humans naturally drift toward good or evil?

When I chose to focus on a distorted understanding of love while dismissing or ignoring justice, I was a perpetually good and kind person, wearing the appropriate Christian badge, yet living as if God did not exist. A practicing atheist.

As Catholic theologian Scott Hahn points out, "You can either draw the will up to the higher truths or drag your intellect down to the lower goods. Ultimately, atheism isn't a lack of evidence; it is a rationalization for indulging in the kind of behavior that we crave. So we use self-seeking rationality to eradicate God's moral law."

I used "brilliant" self-seeking rationality. I'd wait for someone else to make a mistake—any mistake—then use it to transition from whistleblower to lawmaker.

If Ashley seemed disrespectful, dismissive, or stubborn, I puffed myself up with pride, thinking, *At least I don't treat her the way she treats me*, or *How hypocritical*. Then I'd proceed to act out, sporting a cloak of invisibility. The moment my perception of her shortcomings led to a justification of my sins, I was my own cowardly god, slowly converting our covenant to a fragile contract—like a five-year-old screeching, "Well, well, she started it!"

If anything went wrong in life, I magically transformed. No longer subject to God, but only subject to myself. After all, I couldn't rely on anyone—only myself. I only trusted myself and my laws. It only took error (which, without absolutes, is eternally subjective) on anyone's part, and I became miraculously free to walk into heaven on my own terms.

The path of least resistance.

God understands, right? RIGHT?

How clever I was to merge competing forces. I could have my devil's food cake and eat it, too, as if shouting, "Heads I win, tails you lose" while playing Pascal's wager.

Evermoving Thresholds

Like the decades-long sober man instructed by his doctor he *needs* to have a glass of red wine each night to help prevent coronary artery disease, I loved excuses which squeezed my foot, then leg, then body through the door. From the outside, the door shut as a repetitive onslaught of Biblically contrary rationalizations formed a chair under the knob. *I might as well justify staying here*, I probably thought.

Inside, I heard, "Men are visual! Men are visual!" Euphoria welled up inside when one of my addictions was validated. It was "You are now free to move about the cabin" on steroids. The restriction was finally lifted! Thank the Lord I could unfasten my belt, lower my tray, turn on Wi-Fi, and order a Jack and Coke.

My mind took any sliver—any morsel—of margin and ran with it, especially those which were "scientifically proven"— anything that allowed for the most minor relief. My mind conveniently did this with all my favorite sins, creating ladders with progressively addictive rungs.

Whether alcohol, masturbation, caffeine, or comfort food, I'd reason the same: *This relieves anxiety* or *I deserve this* or *I can do whatever I want*. These internal sentences, however, soon desired to become paragraphs, then chapters. If I resisted them for any period of time, I would inevitably scan society for "rational"

3. Epiphany: Works Of The Flesh

outlets to end my latest attempt at discipline. *Ah, there's an article about men's physical needs. Research shows masturbation relieves stress and lowers prostate cancer risk (you don't want to die, do you?). There's an advertisement for fine wine and cheese. Thank God there's a Starbucks next door—but I can't just use the restroom without making a purchase. That would be unethical.* "I'll have a grande vanilla latte with an extra shot—and a slice of coffee cake—and a cake pop." *Caffeine is good for my vessels...or something.*

I had not considered how bra advertisements led to swimsuit issues led to *Playboy* led to online pornography and frequent masturbation; how a few sips of alcohol led to a six-pack led to a dozen shots led to blackout drunkenness; how a few sips of caffeine led to a few cups of coffee led to espresso led to energy drinks; how a few pieces of chocolate led to a half package of marshmallows led to a half tray of brownies led to inhaling a canister of whipped cream chased by a latte in a parking lot; how an innocent game of Snake led to Angry Birds led to weather updates, emails, YouTube, texting, and NBA highlights led to full-on technology idolatry. My childhood and teenage curiosity became adult debauchery.

In his book *Confessions*, Saint Augustine of Hippo conceded, "The first course delighted and convinced my mind, the second delighted my body and held it in bondage."

Paragraph 1865 in the *Catechism of the Catholic Church* states:

> Sin creates a proclivity to sin; it engenders vice by repetition of the same acts. This results in perverse inclinations which cloud conscience and corrupt the concrete judgment of good and evil. Thus sin tends to reproduce itself and reinforce itself, but it cannot destroy the moral sense at its root.

It always progressed from abstinence to mild use; mild to

moderate use; moderate to insatiable and gluttonous use. Regardless of what I digested, it led to absolute indulgence—and boy, did I pay for it. My brain expended all its energy trying to figure out my next move. There was occasional remorse (I think), knowing I went too far even by my increasingly skewed standards. This was a cooling-off, resetting, or detoxification period. A form of self-preservation and likely the very thing hissing to me, *You're doing fine—at least you know when to stop.* But was I stopping or just coasting through yellow lights? If neither, I was certainly speeding through intersections, glancing up to ensure a camera wasn't catching my facial expressions.

As Venerable Fulton Sheen said on *Life is Worth Living*, his 1950s television show:

> There is a repression of reason and moral law very often in order to express the lower instincts, and the argument that such an abnormal person will give is, "Well it's natural, isn't it? Shouldn't one follow one's nature?" Certainly, one should! But what is our nature? Our nature is not that of a goat! Or a pig! Our nature is rational. We're human beings! Governed not by the subconscious mind; governed by a reason and governed by a will. And it is false to say we can always cure a psychological complex by a physiological outlet.

In my worst moments, whispers circled, choking any semblance of regret, allowing my favorite sins to appear nearly innocent: *At least you're not shooting heroin or sleeping with prostitutes.* As if my forms of escaping reality, filling voids, and sidestepping God's commands were somehow better.

Regardless of where I landed, with every episode of gorging and decadence, victimhood comforted and convinced me to remain selfish, ready to escape upcoming challenges. No matter

the intensity, a buzz accompanied all sin. A strong buzz was sought after resetting; a stronger buzz was chased when a strong buzz no longer cut it; and a strongest buzz was hunted when a stronger buzz fell short. Three weeks on, one week off; two months on, four days off; three days on, one day off. No matter the category of sin, I never had a grasp of self-control. I was attempting to catch an eel with oil-soaked hands.
    Rebellion won. It always won, even if incrementally.

A Malformed Thesis

I continued this process as often as I liked, with as much flexibility as I liked, until I found a Bible translation I liked, or until I found "conflicting" verses that provided an opening for sin to thrive. After all, an apparent contradiction cancels itself out, right? To a cunning layman it does.
    For example, I reasoned, *The Bible never outrightly says masturbation is wrong. But I have heard people reference "the body is a temple." Also, masturbation is essentially sex with yourself. Oh, well—if it was so important, wouldn't the Holy Spirit ensure such a large topic was explicitly covered? Hmm....*
    Nevertheless, I'm sure I'd have found another, "more important" verse to smother it anyway. *Hey, wait, the Bible does say a wife and husband rule over each other's bodies, right? The NIV translation says the wife yields her body to her husband. So, reasonably, in the absence of this, masturbation must be encouraged. After all, the only time sex should be avoided is during a time of mutual consent—which has never happened. So that's settled. I should become a theologian! I cracked the code!*
    Even while periodically abstaining from pornography, masturbation was perfectly okay in my mind. I'm sure I thought, *There's no way this is wrong. I clearly haven't gone blind (certainly not physically), as they used to joke about at school. Sure, I need a*

break from my phone screen, but I can think whatever I want, right? I'm not looking, just picturing. See, I do care.

And just like that: an Eddie-made doctrine. A self-interest necessity disguised as virtue.

I also must have occasionally reasoned the impossible: *masturbation can be detached from lust and selfishness.*

Regardless of my internal rationale, I never viewed pornography as a betrayal but as a response to Ashley's refusal and rejection of me. And if not betrayal, it was entirely within my rights to do whatever necessary to fulfill my natural impulses. Resulting damage did not register—ever! Probably because my plan was to carry it to the grave. I must have thought actions couldn't hurt if they were only in secret.

The best part: Ashley said she wasn't refusing or rejecting me (definitely not the way I thought), but that she was nervous and wondered why my love for her was absent. I was covertly investigating verses about conjugal rights rather than exploring how husbands are called to love their wives. My love for her was highly conditional at best and non-existent at worst.

What should have been black and white was grayish to me. Within margins of gray were a half dozen gradients. Compared to black or white, a variant of gray was purple. Then, of course, a half dozen purple variants arose. Compared to the original gray, they might as well have been toasters or peacocks. Because I disregarded God, my decisions got poorer, while my camouflage got richer. As Saint Augustine said, "The punishment of every disordered mind is its own disorder."

Eventually, I was left with an amalgamation of pride, shame, cowardice, and arrogance. Upset with this chaotic reality, I was half-tempted to create yet a new color, unique for my present situation—until my desires and confusions gained more intensity,

3. Epiphany: Works Of The Flesh

then the process reset, and I'd look to redefine my so-called color, sprinting further and further from sacrifice.

However, somewhere I knew of God's nature to liberate, not enslave, humans; yet, surrendering to Him seemed as difficult as crossing Niagara Falls on a tightrope. I could not fathom how He paired unconditional love with discipline, so I collected excuses in a quiver. When I'd feebly reach for an arrow, I'd pull out phrases: *You're justified—go ahead; No one expects perfection; I'm sure everyone else does the same thing; Why does God ask you to face temptations only for you to have to resist them? What does it prove? Why do you even have intense desires if you're meant to control them? If certain actions are so excusable because of teenage hormones, what about adult hormones?*

This mindset was timely when considering one of God's most fundamental directives: sex is designed for one-flesh marriage and primarily ordered toward procreation and life-long unity. The Bible makes this abundantly clear across the Old and New Testaments, yet I easily warped or outright ignored this teaching in an effort to justify or dismiss sexual sin altogether, acting like laws collapsed on themselves when I felt victimized. Add some doses of trauma and "It's natural!", and my reasoning became impenetrable.

So, I did what any disillusioned, prideful, guilty party would do: I created my own absolute truth, while living like there's no such thing as absolute truth. While sprinting from authority, I made Scripture submit to my will. I scoured the internet and studied Bibles to discover opinions that closely resembled mine—unsurprisingly, I easily found them. I chased synonyms, commentaries with multiple interpretations, and those who had their own "modern" versions of Scripture, morals, and values. It's where I found "ironclad" verses to back ever-lenient theories.

There were "Christian" books endorsing every sexual practice known to man; therapists who encouraged pornography within marriage (i.e. with mutual consent, defilement is left to the couple's interpretation); and, like a dog chasing its tail, Bible translations that rendered God's directives softer and softer (lest the Christian community be judged for bigotry until it perfectly matches Society's Ever-Mutable Laws).

To adhere to the world's conclusions, Christianity must adjust, right? Decrees must subtly become a disease; discipline must be seen as oppressive. 2 Peter 3:16 warns of this: "There are some things in them hard to understand, which the ignorant and unstable twist to their own destruction, as they do the other Scriptures."

I found people just like me researching just like me, who led more people just like me into a chasm of Biblical relativism (similar to *creeping gradualism*, a term used by Kitty Werthmann regarding Nazi Germany's steady, calculated takeover of Austria).

The Bible is *your* oyster.

This twisting of Scripture allowed my conscience to breathe happily, even if yet again seared with an iron and reconfigured by shame. After all, I was only committing digital infidelity—the kind where I cheated with dozens of women without the burden of secret texts, phone calls, and miscellaneous cash withdrawals.

Even when I felt I wasn't committing the most commonly judged or ridiculed sins, I did not want to be corrected. I was a self-professed Christian unwilling to surrender my life, so I effortlessly rejected clear Biblical definitions of sin. I say "clear" in hindsight; I was blissfully defiant. Mental gymnastics aside, God's commands were obvious; especially regarding those related to sexual behavior, there was no excuse. I used convenient, encouraging verses from the very epistles that exposed my sins and called for contrition, yet was selective in my seeing and hearing.

Whenever sexual sin was mentioned at a church service, it was vague. The common phrase—"Maybe you're looking at

3. Epiphany: Works Of The Flesh

things you shouldn't be looking at..."—was often wedged between other sins like drug abuse and greed. Because I assume discussing such issues at length was too shameful (even without kids in the congregation), kindred sinners could get "real" in small, private gatherings. Group-confessionals, if you will. Societies, clubs, groups, etc. It made sense at the time. Who wants to feel naked among those who don't sin the way you do?

Because I did not want to get tackled holding a football of disgrace, any mention of sexual sin was passed laterally to other men. *Those guys need help, not me.* I'm not sure what I was thinking—maybe, *As long as it's not with an actual person, I'm fine.* Oddly, when recalling the times pornography was discussed at church, I can't picture myself sitting next to Ashley. I must have mentally left the building.

Like church, the Bible was great when it suited me. When it didn't, I easily rationalized and excused sexual immorality: *I am visual and have needs my wife does not understand*; drunkenness: *I'm traumatized*; and lying: *I need to protect myself from rejection.*

Saint Augustine stated, "If you believe what you like in the gospel, and reject what you don't like, it is not the gospel you believe, but yourself."

Saint Bernard of Clairvaux added, "He who constitutes himself his own master, becomes the disciple of a fool."

Conjuring loopholes in my head was comforting. I started with temptation, then objectification, then masturbation, then cohabitation, then fornication, with an overarching theme of adultery via lust. Rinse and repeat. I matured from crawling to sprinting without much effort. It didn't take much creativity—only a gateway and a deviant mind. Quite easy when everything is viewed as a contract, at best.

Alone, with my Bible alone, my interpretations were all that mattered. An inch, a foot, a yard, a mile.

I praised God while engaging in the opposite of His commands.

"All is vanity and a striving after wind" (Ecclesiastes 1:14).

Screen Actors Guilt

I was an actor. Outwardly—at work, in church, at home—I played leading and supporting roles. In any setting, my primary job was to twist perceptions and reject transparency.

Whether future-scheduling emails to send during dinner so it appeared I was working extra hours, erasing a classmate's name on his art and presenting it as my own, or pretending everything was okay at home with Ashley and I, my role recurred. No matter the circumstances, I would not break character.

For example, I'm a slow runner. Always have been. Throughout high school—whether at basketball or tennis practice—I finished last during running drills. Because it was so humiliating, and because teammates love to tease each other over any shortcoming, I began to dramatically swing my arms during sprints. I wanted my coaches to assume I was trying my hardest, even if I wasn't. I also wanted my teammates to know, *I might be slow, but can't you see how much I care?*

However, no matter how much I flailed—or changed my facial expressions—I remained slow. The same was true of jumping. Even with an "advanced" plyometrics program and special shoes, Jumpsoles, my vertical remained under twenty-two inches. I looked like an idiot sprinting, hopping, and skipping around my parent's driveway with bulky foam high heels. I think they were purchased the same month we got a Ronco Electric Food Dehydrator for four easy payments of $14.99 (plus S&H). Attempts at homemade beef jerky and dried apple snacks, much like attempts at building eversion muscles and toe flexors, left much to be desired.

3. Epiphany: Works Of The Flesh

Yet, after six months of infrequent training, I dunked! The rim was several inches below regulation, and I used a tennis ball, but in my mind I was competing in an NBA dunk contest. So, when asked if I could ever dunk, I would say "Yeah," knowing the sad extent of my lie.

These roles carried just the right amount of pride. Just enough to ensure I never changed my character's clothes.

- Approaching our church, I'd tell myself: *Smile! You're happy to be here.*
- In business meetings: *Smile, act like you've been here before...make sure you drop names (even if you hardly know the people).*
- Approaching the house: *Smile, act normal, she won't notice a thing.*
- In church: *Lift your hands, otherwise people will judge you...they'll know something is wrong.*

It was the same with friends, only it manifested as one-upmanship. I couldn't stop it. I'd often have comments in the queue, await a conversation pause, then insert some exaggerated story about work or my past.

Forbidden Adulthood

"But sin, finding the opportunity in the commandment, wrought in me all kinds of covetousness. Apart from the law sin lies dead" (Romans 7:8).

Adam and Eve had many options. The number of trees in the Garden of Eden is unknown, but one can assume the food on each was the most appetizing ever found on earth. And yet, even though before original sin, God's command calling out *one* specific tree framed it the most appealing—even though it led to death.

Throughout childhood and into my teenage years, I often heard and read: ADULT SHOW. Whether via rabbit ears, basic cable, or satellite, the term *adult show* was intriguing and its meaning heightened. The inference being: *once you're of age, you should be able to process everything on screen, whether sexual, violent, or paranormal.*

Becoming an adult made sin acceptable or, at least, much more tolerable. Yet, I never found a teaching with a clause stating, *Flee from sexual immorality until your culture deems you an adult. Everyone—except adults—who looks at a woman with lust has already committed adultery with her in his heart.*

Along the way, my conscience was scrambled by what I saw as commonplace. However, I realized *adult show* or *adult movie* became permissible consumption of filthy language, sexual immorality, fits of rage, envy, slander, gossip, and idolatry. Sin was crouching at the parental-guideline door. TV-PG, TV-14, and TV-MA were essentially labeled: TV-WatchALittleSin, TV-BeTemptedBySin, and TV-LiveOutSin. No different than abstinence turned gluttony or temptation turned adultery. The enemy—acting as sin's drip line—lulled me to sleep with calculated doses of desensitization. Pretty crafty.

Adult was hypnotic; I could not wait to "mature" and boldly watch sinful behavior on screen. Unsurprisingly, I was impatient. I snuck here, peeked there; I crept in, slipped out.

Shadowed by a chorus of scientific studies, blogs, and newscasts all proving my sin excusable, a subtle hiss confirmed: "Surely you will not die."

Fig Leaves

As my "excusable" vices drove me further into a marsh of shame, I gradually desired to look presentable—even regal. I showered in false affirmation and combed my hair with false acceptance.

3. Epiphany: Works Of The Flesh

For such an exercise, social media was my preferred train wreck. When staying in touch with family and old coworkers, it was innocent enough. However, this represented less than five percent of my usage. If I posted a photo of a lake, sunset, or the beach, I reveled in comments and likes; if I posted a photo of my kids and/or Ashley, the same—only with added weight. I counted the number of likes I received (and from whom, sure to consider their influence, as if some people's *likes* were really worth ten). And if it was a photo of me alone or with a celebrity at an event, I needed extra praise—anything to reinforce status.

Whether I posted on Instagram, Facebook, or LinkedIn, I obsessively refreshed my screen to see who and how many had *liked* me. This allowed me to predict a final tally and percentage of total followers engaged. My day job as a marketer, where I oversaw social media, helped me master this *self-obsession* metric. If these equations worked for a business, they would certainly work for me. As I inwardly focused, my sin justification gained enormous strength, creating new rungs.

With LinkedIn specifically, I regularly checked my profile. I read and reread my employment progression, promotions, personal statement of capabilities, and endorsements—both received and given. I always checked the section "People who viewed your profile also viewed..." Seeing executives listed there overwhelmed me with anticipation. As featured titles increased and decreased, my emotions did the same. My identity relied on how I related to—and how many degrees away I was from—the cream of the crop. My aspirations were not tied to impacting companies, but to how my ego could climb the corporate ladder of prestige, money, and applause.

From this, pretentiousness arose, then metastasized. No doubt it carried to my spiritual life. My brain perversely welded job success to virtue. I'm sure it spilled out of me, depending on who was around. The teachings of C. S. Lewis and Dante complete a picture describing competing forces: animal self and diabolical self. Animal self represents warm-hearted sins of the flesh (lust and gluttony), whereas diabolical self— which Lewis refers to as "the worse of the two"—represents cold-blooded sins of the spirit (pride and envy). From this, Lewis concludes, "a cold, self-righteous prig who goes regularly to church may be far nearer to hell than a prostitute. But, of course, it is better to be neither."

Housed in warm and cold categories, I comprehensively sinned, knowing something was tragically wrong. And so, I continued sewing patches on my Letterman Jacket covering.

In Max Lucado's book, *You Are Mine*, a lowly wooden character named Punchinello desires boxes and balls—lots of them—because society (inhabited by Wemmicks) has deemed them of high value. As the story progresses, Punchinello eventually sells everything he owns in order to buy more boxes and balls than the next guy. As the quantity of items gives way to the quality of items, chaos ensues in the Wemmick village. As Punchinello feverishly follows the rest of the village up a hill (because now it's not only about quantity and quality; it's about how high you can climb while holding your boxes and balls), he gets lost, then trips and falls face first in his maker's workshop. The following plays out:

> "Punchinello." Eli's voice was calm and deep and kind.
>
> The Wemmick still didn't move. He could feel his wooden face turning red.
>
> "Looks like you've been carrying a big load."
>
> The weary Wemmick climbed to his knees but kept his head low.
>
> "These are my boxes and balls," he said quietly.

3. Epiphany: Works Of The Flesh

"Do you play with the boxes and balls?" asked Eli.

Punchinello shook his head.

"Do you like boxes and balls?"

"I like the way they make me feel."

"And how do they make you feel?"

"Important," Punchinello answered, still with a small voice.

"Hmmm," Eli observed, "so you've been thinking like the other Wemmicks. You've been thinking that the more you have, the better you are, and the happier you'll be."

"I suppose so."

While in the marsh of shame, I could've captured millions of likes and comments, garnered a CMO position, and been labeled *TIME* Person of the Year, and would have remained unfulfilled.

Glass House of Cards

Within minutes of receiving my bachelor's degree from Fresno State, my biggest supporter—one of my graphic design professors—approached me in the most tranquil area on campus: Peace Garden.

"Eddie, congratulations! So, what's the plan? Where have you applied?"

I sheepishly answered, "I'm staying at my current job, selling construction supplies."

His confused stare yelled at me: *You are an idiot! You just went through years of training and are deciding to leave it behind?*

After an uncomfortable pause, I continued, "They provide career growth." (*How unique is that?*)

He responded, "Well, best of luck," as he turned to greet other graduates who had undoubtedly prepared better answers.

I was horrible at graphic design, and as many fellow students reminded me, my severe color blindness was a handicap. I only had confidence in one distinct area: illustrating in pen and black ink. No other colors, ever—unless an assignment forced me. These fears of failure and judgment were launchpads to additional victimhood. I could turn anything into a *woe is me* opportunity.

Stubbornly, once I completed a semester or two, I committed to finish, even knowing my trade would be dead to me the minute I graduated.

My degree served as a piece of paper and two centered lines on a resume. Yet, to preserve some dignity, I often lied, saying, "I've done some freelance work" or "Graphic design is a hobby for me."

Upon graduating, I was promoted to assistant general manager, then, within a few months, promoted to general manager. Eighteen months later, another promotion. I confidently accepted the opportunity to run a store three times larger.

Along with several other area stores, we obliterated our January goal, triggering a celebration from everyone in the district. But, once the second month began, my branch was suddenly on an island and I was out of my league. The phones infrequently rang, a massive order was returned, our inventory counts were drastically off, and within the first two weeks, I projected a revenue goal shortage of twenty to thirty percent. So, I panicked, immediately considering a job change. Up to that point, employment had been a constant; I'd not had a gap of unemployment since I was eighteen. If I was going to bow out, I needed a replacement—fast! The fear was so strong I decided to take any

3. Epiphany: Works Of The Flesh 47

job as long as it saved me from imminent failure. Within a week, before the disastrous month had ended, a series of interviews were arranged.

Without any thought, I accepted a position and moved three hours away to Napa. A sales job, no less. I had just proven I did not have the perseverance to be a consistent salesman, yet I was now an outside representative covering a large region in California. Not the height of ignorance, but darn close.

A salesman remains steady regardless of monthly quotas or the unpredictable ebbs and flows of business. But once again, roughly eleven months into my stint, I was about to fall considerably short of my goal. When the sales report reached the team, my row was highlighted the brightest red I'd ever seen in Excel. In last place, I had single-handedly ruined the team revenue average. The humiliation reminded me of an old professor laughing at one of my assignments ("This person doesn't know the basics of color!") and my basketball coach calling me out after a game ("What the hell were you thinking, Trask?!"). So, I did what I had just done a year earlier: I quit. However, this time, I didn't have a substitute. That summer, I sat around Ashley's apartment playing *Street Fighter II Turbo* as Ken—my alter ego in a time of crisis. I had returned to my teenage years.

This mindset followed me from job to job, title to title. Regardless of the money I earned, I over-performed for some short amount of time (usually one to two years), then bailed if I sensed business was going south. I rejected employers before they rejected me.

I tried so hard to be the do-it-all shining star. The standard I had set became impossible to maintain, dramatically exposing my weaknesses. I found myself cornered—forced to make excuses. I'd often go home and complain to Ashley, fashioning myself into a new kind of victim. She questioned my motives a few times but ultimately landed on my side because she trusted my judgment. I always blamed my employers and coworkers because they *didn't care as much as I did*. As in tennis, it was easier to play doubles because a fall guy was next to me. "I told you to rush the net!"

My fear of genuine communication buried Ashley and me. I knew only one speed and never stopped to reflect on my approach to business and lack of self-introspection. Unsurprisingly, as I bailed one situation, my next employer increased my salary because I was transitioning on a collective high note—which became my only negotiation method. I demonstrated short-term results (even if the most recent month was a failure) and generated excitement about my ability to produce quick revenue. To the outside world and to the employer I was leaving, it seemed like "Eddie is climbing the ladder" or "Eddie is going places." I heard variations of this over the years, much to my delight.

Punchinello knows what I'm talking about.

Earlier in *You Are Mine*, he had abandoned and sold everything—including his house—in order to buy more boxes and balls. In one image, perhaps the most heartbreaking, Punchinello rests under a makeshift house: a pile of his prized boxes and balls.

> So what if his arms ached? So what if he kept walking into walls? So what if he had no friends? He had boxes and balls, and when he passed Wemmicks, they would turn and say, "Wow, he must be a good Wemmick." Punchinello heard them. He couldn't see them, but he heard them, and he felt good. *I'm a good Wemmick*, he thought.

As I climbed ladders, I found myself taking first-class flights, meeting celebrities, having meals with CEOs and presidents, drinking some of the finest wine in the world at Michelin-rated restaurants, and attending prestigious functions (including my childhood dream: an NBA Finals game). Yet, despite it all, I was

3. Epiphany: Works Of The Flesh

anxious. I often thought, *Do I belong here? Do I fit in? How can this be? I'm still a novice—how did I get here?* The friction between overconfidence and insecurity was overwhelming. I didn't know who I was. Yet, my arrogant half felt deserving of respect and acceptance. And if either were absent, even if momentary, vices were not only excusable, they were a given.

Feelings of accomplishment, regardless of their strength, often diminished during interviews. Explaining how and why I jumped from job to job was like solving overlapping puzzles. *But every strikeout will get me closer to a home run*, I rationalized. I remained a salesman of sorts, as I had been in my private life, always finding a way to excuse my mistakes. Explaining four, five, or six job hops with sound reasoning without throwing employers under the bus (although I'm sure I did a few times), while keeping stories straight and convincing the employer interviewing me that I wouldn't do the same to them was ridiculously tiring. This was probably the main reason I didn't land most of the jobs I interviewed for—my stories and judgment were losing credibility. During my ten-year wine industry stint, I easily met with over fifty prospective employers and networked with an additional hundred. Each official and informational interview was accompanied by obsessive preparation and research. I reasoned: *I need to connect all these decisions in a logical way.*

■ ■ ■

Six weeks before my confession to Ashley, on July 21, my last wine job ended. After my employer motioned for me to join him outside, I knew he intended to discuss something serious—likely the end of my contract. As we sat under a canopy in the most tranquil area on the property, I was told what I already knew: my performance had plateaued. There was not much to defend, so I sat and listened. We exchanged a few congratulatory words about our time together. A few weeks shy of my three-year commitment, our chapter closed. Sadly, had we forgone a contract, I would've bailed a year earlier—right on cue.

I drove home and told Arlo I'd be home for about ten days, pompously thinking I'd secure a job in a few days, then take a week off before starting. I hugged Ashley and told her everything would work out.

"I know it will," she responded. "I trust you."

By the end of the day, I had an interview scheduled for the following day with the owner of one of the largest privately-run wineries in Napa Valley. Despite the excitement, I knew I needed some sort of break—but from what?

I didn't want to know.

4. DEATH TO SELF: CALAMITY

Submit yourselves therefore to God. Resist the devil and he will flee from you. Draw near to God and he will draw near to you. Cleanse your hands, you sinners, and purify your hearts, you men of double mind. Be wretched and mourn and weep. Let your laughter be turned to mourning and your joy to dejection.

—James 4:7-9

Since therefore Christ suffered in the flesh, arm yourselves with the same thought, for whoever has suffered in the flesh has ceased from sin, so as to live for the rest of the time in the flesh no longer by human passions but by the will of God.

—1 Peter 4:1-2

Now three days after my confession to Ashley, I had a lunch interview scheduled with a director of one of the largest wine corporations in the world. She insisted I go.

Two minutes from the restaurant parking lot, new shame stabbed me: I recalled an incident from a few months earlier when I was at an out-of-town event, horribly drunk, flirting with a woman, and exaggerating that I ran a winery. As she left, I followed her and her friend, attempting to join their private shuttle back to a hotel.

I shouted to myself, *Why now?! Why these thoughts now?* However—only a few days removed from my initial outpouring—I understood when God wanted me to expose something else, however untimely. Searing pain was a given.

Recalling that night was debilitating. Part of me knew it was an issue, yet I relegated it to an alternate universe with no access. Now with heightened clarity, my drunkenness and sexually immoral proclivities practically induced vertigo. Still, I wondered, *Am I sick because of remorse or fear of confession?*

"How do you handle stress?" the interviewer asked.

"What is your greatest weakness?"

"Why are you the right person for this role?"

"Name a time you were faced with an obstacle—how did you respond?"

I'm surprised I didn't throw up on the table.

The questions continued for forty-five minutes. As I sensed the conversation improving, I caught a second wind. I had become confident and animated only to shrink back to defeated and deflated within minutes. I still didn't know who I was. My act was over, yet I insisted on stepping in front of the curtain as it lowered. I badly wanted the job, but no training in the world would've produced a believable routine that day. Despite the best answers and resumé I could produce, the interviewer saw a crumbling, distraught man.

At the end of our meal, we smiled, shook hands, and he added, "I'd be happy to stay connected and help you navigate the complexities of wine conglomerates, but your experience does not match what we're looking for. I'm sorry. Here's my business card. Let's stay in touch."

4. Death To Self: Calamity

I left the restaurant staring at my shoes. The drive home was fifteen minutes, but it felt like two. Numbly suspended a foot above rock bottom, I didn't know if I had ascended or descended to that position.

Clear the Decks

Back at home, Ashley was packing her bags. As soon as I walked in, she looked up with an obligatory question: "How did the meeting go?"

"Garbage," I said, as I headed to our bedroom to comfort myself into a hoodie, sweatpants, and Kirkland Signature athletic socks (also known as "Cathy Socks"—my cousin placed a pair in each year's Thanksgiving gift bag). Because conviction overcame me, I proceeded to tell her of my newly remembered shame. It was our non-verbal agreement of sorts: I feel prompted to share, I share. She feels driven to lash out, she stares.

"Yes—I was out of my mind. I don't know what I would've done. When the shuttle driver asked me to provide clearance, I left."

"Seriously? You followed her?" Ashley asked.

"Yes—and I had previously asked a girl to dance. She said no," I said. "And I guess I was chatting with an escort at a bar that same night."

"What? You *guess*?" she asked in shock. "Why?!"

"I didn't know she was an escort. But she was acting nice—a little too nice. She alluded to it after a while. I said no. She left."

Ashley stared with disgust, saying, "This is ridiculous." After a long pause, she continued, "I feel like I don't even know who you are."

She then began frantically searching for an accountability app. We had decided it was best for her to visit her friend, Melissa, for the weekend, and Ashley desired to put a few measures in place before leaving. Having drunk from a fire hose of sin for the past three days, trust was dead. We agreed that giving her remote access to my phone was warranted. However, after installation, the app failed multiple times. I assured her I would be fine, but each word was meaningless. Understandably, I could do nothing to console her.

She left with a blank expression and a "See you later." I'm sure she was happy to escape the Eddie Confessional, if only for two days.

The kids and I stood at the front window, watching her spill into her car. I only recall her profile as she drove off. Atypical, but reasonable.

"Where is Mommy going?" Arlo asked as I rushed to find a teddy bear for Eviana.

Disoriented, I spastically turned my head from the hall to the living room to the kitchen.

"She's going to visit a friend. She'll be back soon, buddy," I responded.

Within twenty minutes, the kids were down for their naps. I called my friend Mike, who, having just landed a dream job, was in the process of moving from Maine to Ohio. We met in 2006 at an old company retreat. At the time, we were both struggling with faith and maturity. Over the years, as we grew closer, we shared bits and pieces of our lives, but always withheld the most shameful. He had never explicitly said it, but I knew he and his wife had gone through something catastrophic. I guessed it was largely sexual in nature, so I took a chance and spilled my guts, revealing all relevant details. I hoped he would share his journey.

"Did you cheat on her?" he asked.

"No. I mean, not in-person, if that's what you're asking," I responded.

"Okay. It's just good to know if this was an affair," he answered.

"I understand. So, yeah, I have told her a number of things:

4. Death To Self: Calamity

pornography, drinking, flirting, and other random stuff," I said, refusing to mention my Obsessive-Confession Disorder.

"How is she taking it?" he asked.

"It's tough to tell right now. Most of it is restrained. She is a *cooler-heads-prevail*-type person...I think."

"Okay. This is going to take a lot of work, but I am a testament to God's redemptive power," he said. "Seriously, whatever you need, call me. Find at least one other guy who can help you with this. I have a friend who went through something similar. I'll introduce you two, if that's okay."

Mike's voice grew serious as he prayed for me and reiterated his availability as an emergency hotline. He then reciprocated vulnerability and shared his old secret lifestyle. Portions of our stories were analogous, while others showcased personality, childhood, and spiritual differences. Nevertheless, I had a confidant.

The rest of the weekend was awful. For the first time in our relationship, Ashley chose to be separated from me, several hours away, praying with Melissa, and coming to terms with betrayal. She even left her wedding ring behind on the nightstand. I was home with the kids, scraping meals together, attempting to genuinely play games, and counting the minutes until bedtime so I could cry out to God. I desperately tried remaining calm. I stared into Arlo's eyes as he explained his latest LEGO creation. I smiled, tearless. Inside, I wailed.

The first night, after bawling my eyes out for twenty minutes, I explored online sermons. I was an infant looking for spiritual milk, and what I found appeared to be laced with poison. Suddenly overcome with darkness and fear, I shut off the TV and turned on the living room and hall lights. The pastor—who was simply standing and talking—terrified me.

Four hours later, just after 1 a.m., Ashley called in a panic, having felt darkness creeping into her room.

"I need help! I don't want to wake up Melissa," she said, frightened.

"What's wrong?" I asked as I sat up and positioned pillows against the wall.

She replied, "I feel like something's in my room. There's just this...this evil. I was trying to ignore it for a while, but it kept getting stronger. Then I felt like something was trying to choke me, and I couldn't control my eyes. They just started freaking out! I was saying, 'No, no, no', but it didn't work. I was praying and praying, and it let up. I turned on the flashlight on my phone and started playing worship music, but it's not helping. I'm too scared to get out of bed and get Melissa. I don't know what else to do. Can you please pray?"

"Okay.... Father, in the name of Jesus, please scatter the enemy. Please remove this from Ashley's room. Please take over. Lord, we pray for restful sleep. We pray for your strength. Help us.... In Jesus' name, Amen." I didn't know what I was doing, but for a few minutes, we were strangely bonded, however unhealthy the circumstances.

I shook my head, realizing I had never prayed over us.

Despite my petitions to God, we both went to sleep with trepidation. The feeling was familiar to both of us. As prayer ends, our brains tend to fixate on everything that led to the prayer in the first place.

In tears, she arrived home Sunday afternoon. Amazingly, we hugged, yet were strangers. I was relieved to be in her presence, but the haze, anger, and sadness were unmistakable.

That night I researched local therapists and articles about how to be a better Christian husband. I also signed up for a November marriage retreat. It couldn't come fast enough.

It was time to be a new kind of man.

Tempest

Beginning Monday, nearly a week after confession, I began journaling. My last exposure had been in first or second grade when I had a diary with a cartoon dinosaur on it. I remember writing a few words to accompany drawings of an ice cream cone, the sun, and a girl in my class. For decades thereafter—because written thoughts seemed pointless to me—doodling had been my favorite form of therapy.

I also resolved to pray with Ashley every night. We wrote down Bible verses on note cards we believed would help combat any attack, having learned we were in for a unique ride. Ashley offered to do most of them. I obliged because my writing is awful, and it would've been stupid to turn down such a kind gesture. *We're going to face this together*, I thought.

Yet, we couldn't possibly know the gravity of the ensuing battle. I was just glad we still lived in the same house.

Then the real purging started.

On the couch with Ashley, we had just put the kids to bed, and I had already confessed another sin. Then, with the weight of traumatic déjà vu, she asked, "What's wrong?"

"I don't know. I need to go to the bedroom. I'll leave the door open," I said, assuring her I wasn't going to revert to old habits.

Out of nowhere, a sexual urge consumed me. My stomach in knots, I expressed my turmoil.

"I have an intense desire to masturbate...or something. This is not usual. It's too much."

Ashley responded, eyes squinted, still wearing betrayal on her sleeve, "*Okay*...."

At a loss, I power-walked to our bedroom to read Bible verses and pray. The impulse intensified. I shifted gears and called Mike.

"I need your help," I said.

"I'm glad you called, man," he replied. "What's wrong? Tell me everything."

"Dude, my body is on fire with overwhelming urges. Why is this happening?" I asked. "I was doing fine, now I feel like I'm losing control. What is this? I have never felt this before. This is so frustrating."

"This is you resisting flesh," he said. "Self-denial is crazy, but God is faithful. Very few people would agree with this, but it is for your own good."

"Okay," I exhaled. "But I've resisted before. I've gone up and down with discipline for most of my life."

Mike continued, "For some reason, this is clearly different. Regardless, set that aside. Start your prayers with a list of what you're grateful for, not complaints about what is missing from your life. Get your focus on Him and off your temptations—voluntary or involuntary. Don't wait."

"And study Ephesians 6," he remembered.

Then we prayed. Disaster averted. An hour later I was back on the couch, explaining everything.

"I called Mike," I said as Ashley curled up with a blanket on the couch, clearly apprehensive.

"Was he helpful?" she hesitantly asked, knowing nothing about such a process. We were equally clueless.

"Yes. Very. He implied he had gone through the same thing," I responded. "He says it's all happening because I'm resisting flesh. I don't know. I have no idea how long this will last."

"Okay. Well, whenever it creeps up on you, let me know, and regardless of the conversation we're having, or what we're busy doing with the kids, go and pray. Don't worry about leaving awkwardly. I know you often say you're fine when you're not. This seems very important."

"Thank you," I said. Then I wondered, *Wouldn't sex solve all of this?*

If only I knew then what I know now.

Don't Give Up the Ship

I fought temptation and torment every night. Whether twenty-five minutes, thirty-five minutes, or over an hour, the goal remained: resist until I can breathe again.

I even fought during the day. I fought whenever I needed to—if driving, I'd turn on worship music; if reading to the kids, a quick *Help me, Father*; if making lunch, *Rejoice in the Lord always...*; if cleaning the garage, *Do not conform....* Regardless of the scenario, if I felt urges, rage, fear, or intimidation, I lifted my spiritual fists. Under constant attack, it was a type of battle I had never fathomed.

As Saint John Cassian wrote, "The demons do not contend with us when we do our own will, for then our wills become devils."

Here we go. Another assault.

In our bedroom, I patiently sat in silence, not forcing regimen, and calmly allowed the Holy Spirit to point me towards which spiritual weapons I should use (e.g. prayer, verse recitation, worship music, etc.).

Sadly, however, they were often loudly disrupted by the enemy.

I absorbed the wildest lies about failure, death, Ashley, my kids, religion, and God. The sniper assailant was secure in a tower, yelling, "Checkmate!" I forcefully, almost indignantly, declared Bible verses to survive each day. Often bawling, I lifted my hands to heaven, asking God to see this through.

Then a new round of confession.

"I left work early and got drunk with some friends. By the time I got home, the buzz had faded enough that you thought I had one to two drinks, not eight. I chewed a ton of gum and avoided conversation as much as possible." *If we had a normal marriage, I could've stumbled in drunk without any concern*, I stupidly thought.

"I almost accidentally screen-mirrored porn onto our TV while you were in the room."

"Yes—I was secretly objectifying you." *I just wanted my wife*, I reasoned. But was that true? Was I driven by love or lust?

"Since my early teenage years, I peeked down shirts, up dresses, through gapes in tank tops, looking to take advantage of any possible wardrobe malfunction, blatant exposure—any opportunity, really. I didn't really try to stop. Yes—you could call that perversion. I couldn't not look."

"Several times, I spent over one hundred dollars on a meal and drinks," I added. "And I paid for women's meals, whether it was a business expense or not. I got joy out of paying for them. It was for attention."

"I took other girlfriends to that restaurant...to that same spot," I sighed.

"And I wasn't honest about how many women I had been with. Clearly, it wasn't just you and one other like I said before."

As vague as I was, Ashley knew exactly what I was saying. Her emotions and expressions no longer communicated anything new.

And just like that, I had returned to the evening of the first confession. A numb, disgusted, dead man walking.

Still, on the couch at the end of each night, grace enabled me to pray two cushions removed from Ashley. She attempted to join, but often dispiritedly slumped, not closing her eyes in fear of falling asleep while I pled for God to help our marriage. I rarely wanted to—it felt like a chore. There were nights I wanted to curl into a ball and never wake. Oh, the child in me, always wanting to escape pain and responsibility—even with new knowledge within me. As in James 4:17: "Whoever knows what

4. Death To Self: Calamity

is right to do and fails to do it, for him it is sin." And John 15:22: "If I had not come and spoken to them, they would not have sin; but now they have no excuse for their sin." Many nights the prayer helped, but surprisingly, it was the act of saying anything in those moments that produced hope, albeit days, weeks, and months later. The choice between speaking and staying silent was enormous. I can't adequately convey what these decisions looked or felt like. Regardless, afterwards, I just wanted rest. Thank God for bedtime.

Then a new round: dreams.

Nightmares, sexual dreams, crippling anxiety, unbelievable torment. And, once awake—you guessed it—a conviction consumed me: *Time to confess.*

"I had a wet dream last night," I said, shaking my head.

"What?" Ashley asked, completely caught off guard. "Did it involve sex? What was going on?"

"No. Well, yes, I guess. I'm not sure," I stammered, as I got increasingly defensive. *What business is it of hers what I dream? Is this even real? Seriously! We're not having sex, and I'm supposed to control my dreams? Why am I being nudged to share this?*

Suffice it to say, she was hurt. This enraged me. *Now I have to be alert when I'm not awake? Yeah, that makes sense. WHAT is going on?*

The dreams were persistent and excruciating, lashing me with humiliation and anger. *Confess my dreams? Seriously?* My reasoning seemed obvious: *Why would any person need to confess such a high level of conscious sins, let alone an intricate level of "subconscious sins"? Why would God want me to confess things out of my control?*

There's no way this is His plan, I thought.

I went to bed most nights praying for dream purity, but many times the prayers were unanswered, and I awoke in a *Twilight Zone* episode. Crippled by despair, I now feared sleep. Little did I know how closely these feelings resembled Ashley's. I couldn't see her, just poor ol' Eddie. In these moments, I cried out to God: "I'm not doing anything!" or "I didn't do anything to invite this!" or "Please stop this process!" The worst came out of me, aimed in all directions: pride, malice, envy, jealousy, and a host of other overpowering emotions—all further demeaning me.

Ashley had fallen in love with a being of my own conjuring—a con man forced into existence by spinelessness. A man now collapsing, forgetting his spouse in the process. I saw it all over her face, which was configured as if to ask, *Seriously, what is wrong with you? I understand you're going through hell, but what about me? Why are you acting like your feelings are more significant? No matter how insane you feel, please see how upside down I feel. I thought I knew the man I was married to! Please don't forget that.*

But I was running scared, blind with every category of excuse, repeating in my head, *How do we shatter the remains of our old relationship while learning to build an entirely new one? All while a spotlight shines on every dot of my soul? Where would this maturity come from? I can't do it. I can't. There's no way hope can be restored.*

Then a whisper from the Holy Spirit: *Keep going.*

Then another round: in public.

My former desensitization was now hyper-sensitization. Temptations were everywhere! I had crossed a now-collapsed bridge. Now barraged by pornographic culture, specific clothing was amplified. At checkout lines, magazines and advertisements were motioning for me. Women everywhere seemed to be whispering, "Come hither." I'd turn a corner, and a very realistic cartoon character on a board game would greet me, dressed in a miniskirt; at another corner, I'd be met by scanty Halloween costumes; another corner, watersports packaging; another corner, headless mannequins in yoga pants and sports bras; another corner, a lingerie display the size of a school bus. Women's bodies were everywhere and on everything. *Why is everything so*

4. Death To Self: Calamity

pronounced now that I'm trying to escape lust? Does this mean I'm a freak? None of this stood out before!

With this newfound reality, I felt I could better justify my past behaviors and excuse future sins. *It's everywhere! I'm drowning in this stuff. How could anyone avoid this ambush?* I felt like Saint Augustine: "I went to Carthage, where I found myself in the midst of a hissing cauldron of lust." And this was all in broad daylight—in a run-of-the-mill, big-box store!

Then came deprecating thoughts: *If you can't function while surrounded by suggestive bras, panties, and bikinis, you're a mutant. No one would agree with you. If you can't handle it, you're the problem. This is all normal.*

Right?

But who defines normal? Hasn't "normal" been on a sliding scale since the beginning of time?

As C. S. Lewis wrote, "In the first place our warped natures, the devils who tempt us, and all the contemporary propaganda for lust, combine to make us feel that the desires we are resisting are so 'natural,' so 'healthy,' and so reasonable, that it is almost perverse and abnormal to resist them."

Even with the knowledge of 1 Corinthians 10:13, ("No temptation has overtaken you that is not common to man. God is faithful, and he will not let you be tempted beyond your strength, but with the temptation will also provide the way of escape, that you may be able to endure it"), I was nauseous. Entrapped and harassed, I felt the attack was inescapable, as if the enemy was saying, *You may mentally remain stationary, but I'm going to physically push you toward sin.* Even with abhorrence from betraying Ashley, there remained a desire to continue peeking at women, now heightened beyond imagination—and with a fire of conviction to confess. Every. Single. Time.

I thought, *This has crossed a major line. Absolutely ridiculous.*

Yet, somehow, grace was at work.

"I looked at a woman's chest. And another woman's butt. And a magazine cover of a topless woman, um, covering herself."

"What does that mean? Did you stare?" she asked.

I thought, *Why do I need to confess this trivial crap? I feel like a child. I don't want to look! It's just happening. I want to get past all this. Is this possibly some strange guilt complex? Is she somehow demoting me every time I confess? No one should have to confess or receive this level of information! Don't all men look at bodies, even if not lusting?*

"No. It was a glance, almost unconscious. It wasn't lust."

Wait, what is lust? When does any specific action become lust? Who is most likely to provide a sound definition?

I added, "It wasn't a double take. It wasn't a stare."

"I don't understand. You're saying it's perfectly normal to glance at a woman's chest (call it a single take) as long as you don't, what...get an erection? When does lust occur?" Ashley asked with full curiosity.

I responded with annoyance, "No, I'm just saying there's a difference between a calculated look and a line of vision."

"Line of vision?" she asked.

Line of vision was something I had invented to stay sane—the instances where I was truly caught off guard and could do nothing to avoid what I saw, aside from entering a store with my eyes plucked out.

"Yes. Where I'd need to live in a cave to avoid it," I added as an excuse.

"I'm so confused," she said.

"Me, too," I said. "This is stupid. I don't know if I'm looking because I still have portions of my old self alive or because this is truly acceptable for men."

But, of course, whether deliberate or accidental, I'd fight to ensure any stimuli did not permeate my brain and somehow appear in my thoughts and dreams. *I can't let my thoughts*

4. Death To Self: Calamity

drift! I belong in a monastery or an asylum. I often returned home overstressed with a headache, having made dozens—if not hundreds—of micro-decisions to reject temptation. I felt as if I had been born in colonial America and caught a time machine to the present day. I was in a cage whether I gazed or not. Pure lunacy.

C. S. Lewis again provides wisdom:

> Those who are seriously attempting chastity [...] soon know a great deal more about their own sexuality than anyone else. They come to know their desires as Wellington knew Napoleon, or as Sherlock Holmes knew Moriarty; as a rat-catcher knows rats or a plumber knows about leaky pipes. Virtue—even attempted virtue—brings light; indulgence brings fog.

Admittedly, even in the light, pride won. *Look at me—I humbled myself; I'm actively fleeing my ego and impurity. I must be doing something right; has anyone else contended with this?*

During this time, out of complete arrogance and stupidity I bet, I hastily attempted thirty-six and seventy-two-hour water-only fasts. I honestly don't know what I was thinking. With virtually no prayer, what was the purpose? Maybe vanity masquerading as virtue?

Ashley approached me as I lay gaunt with my mouth open, my hair the longest it had been since toddlerhood. And since I wasn't working and we weren't intimate, I had no need to shave my sparse, Brillo-Pad beard. "I have something to tell you, but it's really difficult."

"Okay...."

I'm sure I thought, *Finally! Eddie 124, Ashley 1.*

"You remember my friend Oliver?" she asked. "You always felt weird about him, huh?"

"Of course," I said, growing visibly upset.

"We went out a few times before I met you. I should have told you."

"I knew it. I knew something was off. All along you acted like this dude had only been a friend. You guys grabbed coffee together and you expected me to be totally fine with it. You always wanted me to be buddy-buddy with that guy," I added.

Ashley's honesty hit me hard—really hard. The pain was surprisingly new. The agony of confessing and that of receiving a confession were distinctly different. Ten minutes later, she found me praying in our bedroom.

With tears in her eyes, she asked for a hug. "I'm really sorry," she said.

For the first time we exchanged pain. Humbling. Although, secretly, I wanted to prolong this upper hand feeling. I wanted to hold out forgiveness, but God had other plans.

It Was the Lust of Times

I believe Ashley's confessions, regardless of gravity or quantity, allowed my depravity to rear its head again. I pondered, *Now that she's being transparent, that gives me a little margin to not feel like a lunatic. If I look at women, and it's not deliberate, I'm not going to lose my mind. After all, we are all human.*

But just as quickly as small temptations and excuses entered my brain, God pulled me up and reigned me in like I was an impulsive dog, acting as my invisible perimeter. His grace reminded me how ignorant backsliding would be in any increment. *There is no excuse for lust*, I recited, *regardless of circumstances.*

So, with grace guiding me, I turned to logic. Since I am equipped with peripheral vision and intuition, I often sense uncertainty and danger. In an effort to escape the snares of lust,

I made a decision to view sexual temptation as lethal. This enabled me to call audibles and remove myself from many situations. If tempted behind a woman in the checkout line, I moved to another line; if in a grocery-store aisle, the same applied; if seeking a store clerk, I'd choose one dressed modestly; if reading an online article and a provocative ad appeared, I left the webpage; if a jogger was up the road possibly wearing lust-inducing clothing, I avoided looking in her direction. At first, these exercises felt unreasonable, and I knew how stupid they'd sound to the average man or woman. I'd either be seen as a puritan who couldn't function in society or a pervert who couldn't function around women. Nevertheless, as training increased, such exercises became critical to my quest.

The question was, *Why would I need to look?* The choice was no longer to stare or not, to lust or not. The choice was to look or not. This was the root decision. Of course, the world whispered, *As a man, you must look! If you don't look, why, you're not a man at all.*

Previously I had been so deceived that I believed this. But how would objectifying God's creations make me more of a man? That makes zero sense.

Was I ever at a crime scene where I needed to be aware of all people, their clothes, and their height and weight? No. Was the woman I was staring at hoping that some man would come along at a later date to remind her of what she was wearing and what color her clothes were? No. My question remained: *Why did I look?* It was the same as asking, *Why did I lie? Why did I inflate my ego? Why did I indulge?* It was easy, that's why. It didn't take thought or self-control, just action. And if the action is "normal," why would I ever stop? And if "normal" changes daily, I'd conceivably slide into hell as if it's the Promised Land (or, better, the Com-promised Land).

Complete surrender, guided by absolutes, would be the only antidote. But whose version of absolutes?

I remember reading about Vito Bialla, who—at the age of fifty-two—became the first to complete a six-day, *double Ultraman*.

Ultraman is a three-day, 515 km (320 mile) multisport race. Each race is divided into three stages over three days: The first is a 6.2-mile (10-km) ocean swim from Kailua Bay to Keauhou Bay, followed by a 90-mile (145-km) cross-country bike ride, with vertical climbs that total 6,000 feet. Stage two is a 171.4-mile (276-km) bike ride from Volcanoes National Park to Kohala Village Inn in Hawi, with total vertical climbs of 4,000 feet. Stage three is a 52.4-mile (84-km) double-marathon, which starts at Hawi and finishes on the beach at the Old Kona Airport State Recreation Area. Each stage must be completed within 12 hours or less. The swim portion of stage one must be completed in 5.5 hours or less.

When asked how he persevered mentally, Vito answered:

I had so much support and so many people cheering me on I couldn't believe it. Seeing the other athletes, the *ultranuts*, made me feel I was with my species. I learned how to kill negative thoughts the minute they popped up, kill them right then and think about something else. Negative thinking is like a disease. It starts with a wart and turns into a cancer, so you have to kill it right at the onset...it works.

Recalling such a mindset was an immediate blessing. If I entertain thoughts of justified sin, argue I'm not sinning, or assume a simple glance is harmless, I open a door. No matter what Ashley says to me, how bad the day, how dejected I feel, or what society says, my mission remains the same: run the race!

To face what the world believes does not need conquering

4. Death To Self: Calamity

seems idiotic and maybe even self-righteous and arrogant. However, when I revisited Scripture, "shun immorality" echoed in my spirit. What I didn't find was Scripture along the lines of, *flirt with sexual sin, look for worldly answers to your issues, you're only human, feed your desires, embrace your excuses.*

Nevertheless, like every other lesson learned, I knew mistakes would precede accomplishment.

Hanged, Drawn, and Quartered

Ashley and I were often reduced to mental fetal positions while worship music cyclically played in the background. We took this measure to drown out negativity. The kids often saw tears in our eyes. No doubt they felt neglected and insecure for weeks on end. We tried to get out as a family and appear normal, but I doubt our masks were convincing. We hugged a few times and gave even fewer kisses on the cheek, but nothing beyond. The avoidance of sex was understandable because she was so hurt, but it also exacerbated our problems. *I'm supposed to learn self-control at the most foreign level, without any physical outlet, while remaining calm and forgiving? Meanwhile, while I'm struggling to love her, Ashley is supposed to learn how to consistently trust me, forgive me, love me, and remain calm? This is way too much to ask of both of us, yet somehow these parallels are supposed to intersect?*

This was September and October for us. Unbelievably, we always got out of bed to face another day, anticipating further degrees of hell. With constant nausea and heads hung low, we somehow marched forward, day after day after day. As horrible as it was, we somehow trusted that God was directing us.

In the middle of it, I began seeing a therapist named Susan. Her office was peaceful and her restroom was clean. I was so used to seeing poop and pee stains from kids, I smiled when I saw glistening porcelain, lit candles, and a soap dispenser that had more soap inside than out.

Because she valued my time and dissipating money, Susan always avoided chit-chat. We trudged through forgiveness exercises and identified negative thought patterns, agreeing that such training was invaluable.

But, she vehemently disagreed with my habitual confession: "You shouldn't have done that."

"Confession is ideal with a mediator."

"Why are you sharing so much?"

To which I answered, "I understand your point. You're saying we're not equipped to handle the resulting emotions. But it's not like I planned this. The feelings are too strong in the moment. Everything just happened—and continues to happen—on God's terms, or so it seems. Not only that, if I don't tell her, I remain the old Eddie, full of secrets."

Despite the back and forth, we found common ground. Thus, progress was made, but in late October, I told Susan I might not come back due to finances and our upcoming marriage retreat.

■ ■ ■

A week later, Ashley and I were off to the retreat three hours away from home. We paid some friends to stay with the kids all five days. We discussed routines, food choices, and activity ideas—and left them with Ashley's car keys.

Anticipating genuine friendship, I couldn't wait to meet couples who shared comparable lives. Also, tired of my pre- and post-confession disguise, I desired to finally share my *complete* testimony—even if leaving me completely exposed. However, Ashley was mortified, thinking of the vulnerability likely required at such an event.

Within the first few hours, we grew close to one of the three couples at our table. By the end of the first day, we befriended

4. Death To Self: Calamity

another couple. And by the end of the second day, we had all bonded. We each had shared the deepest, darkest secrets of our lives—or so we believed. I spoke for myself, as did Ashley. She told our story so precisely, with so much emotion, I could barely handle it. Its emphasis was on a girl not loved for who she was, and was annoying, needy, and clingy—a girl who wanted a real prince, not a stand-in. Hopelessly clinging to denial, I blankly stared, awaiting the next group activity.

As each couple spilled their guts on the table, the others prayed for and consoled one another. The women often seemed skeptical and unprotected, and the men disrespected and controlled. The sentiment was the same across a room of over sixty couples. During the week, by way of various activities, we got to know couples outside our group. Pornography, infidelity, lying, and an umbrella of confusion were common. I felt secure in the environment but very disturbed by how many of us were bashing our heads against walls.

One night, after all breakout sessions had ended, we sat with the only remaining counselor in the building. Her name was Carol, and she was an angel. The exercise she placed before us sounded simple: Ashley categorically exposes her deep hurts while I learn to listen effectively, then respond to her, paraphrasing what she said in an effort to show I actually understand. Carol suggested saying back to Ashley what she said to me would foster empathy.

In the heart of the exercise, with more sadness than anger, Ashley blurted, "You knew how I felt. You knew it! You did some of the things I feared the most. I had shared all my issues with you. You knew of all my traumas. I told you I felt like an object to you. I need love, not lust!"

"And how does all this make you feel?" Carol asked.

Ready to describe betrayal in the rawest terms, Ashley sat back for a second, sighed, then leaned forward. Her elbows rested on her knees, her hands hugged the sides of her neck, and her face disappeared from view. "Unworthy, unloved, unprotected, violated, worthless, depressed, like trash, lonely, rejected, and abandoned."

Ashamed, I sat in shock for a minute with my hand limp on Ashley's shoulder. The wheels in my head were turning despite tireless enemy sniper attacks.

Finally, I lifted my head and responded, "You believe my disregard and dismissal of your issues kept me selfish, unable to see how my actions were destroying us. You felt unworthy, unloved, depressed, rejected, abandoned...." I turned to Carol. "I don't remember all the feelings, but I understand what I've done."

I looked Ashley in the eyes and apologized.

Carol then turned to her, wanting to ensure I understood the message correctly. "Is that all right?"

"Yes," she said.

Carol smiled. "Guys, this is tough work. I'm proud of you both. Eddie, she has to be able to talk about these feelings. You'll have a chance to discuss yours, but at this moment, the violation of trust needs to be addressed, which means you need to understand her. This is layered."

The night ended with hugs and sighs of relief. Ashley felt she had dropped off a few backpacks of previously unresolved issues. I felt the same because I had never listened this well in my life. Hearing such pain was unnerving, but I knew its exposure was significant to our healing.

The moment the retreat ended, we said goodbye to our friends, then raced to our car and drove 85 mph all the way home, anxious to see our kids.

The choice to leave them for a week was well beyond our capacity. There was no way they were going to understand why we left, regardless of explanation. When we arrived home, Eviana stood at a distance, heartbroken. With tears in his eyes, Arlo rushed to give us bear hugs. As tough as it had been, our decision was validated—albeit barely—by communication improvement. I think we both reasoned that the pursuit of a healthy marriage would benefit the kids long term. Beyond this slight optimism, I only recall a continued horrifying struggle with false hope followed by glimmers of real hope, premature celebrations, passive-aggressive patterns, severe misunderstandings, overwhelming anxiety, doubt, and—as one would guess—many more confessions.

Goliath

During this time, in the midst of continual confusion, I was convicted to never use contraception again. As a child, I was taught about the Catholic Church's teaching on it, but it was buried somewhere within my sin strata. I previously had no qualms with birth prevention. It was so common, I had embraced it with open arms. Ashley was shocked yet almost immediately receptive to the idea. We both saw glimpses of light but couldn't articulate them. We wanted to be rightly ordered to procreation but couldn't articulate that either.

We had no clue God was catechizing us.

Less than a week later, we attempted to be intimate. It was an awkward, delicate dance.

I was overrun with testosterone, and she with fear. My heart appreciated her willingness to even make an attempt. Yet, my body and brain focused on how long it had been since I masturbated, had sex, or knowingly lusted (obviously devoid of comparison to what pre-marital chastity calls for). With that in mind, my love for her was secondary. As I approached her, she was overwhelmingly nervous. As I noticed, I showed some compassion, but even that was secondary. She needed reassurance of my commitment to her, of my love for *all* of her. I needed an escape from all the distress, all the heinous absurdity that I had been fighting for months.

Afterwards, we felt semi-loved and numb. I expected all our problems to vanish; she simply expected progress.

■ ■ ■

December began calm and quiet. I believed the festive season was bringing out our best qualities. Christmas traditions—some original, some old—kept heavy emotions at bay. But, given our history of roller coasters, more issues arose out of nowhere. Backtracking soon became our newest tradition. I couldn't tell the difference between an inability to remember specific details and a purposeful rejection of them. It all equated to perceived secrecy.

"Yeah, I watched when you and the kids were out of the house," I started. Under my breath, I alluded to watching intercourse. Even though I thought I had already disclosed it, shame manifested as cowardly murmurs.

"I thought you said you only saw individual women," Ashley said, visibly upset.

"No, I told you there was an occasional man and woman… and…and…woman and woman," I defended, as I nearly dry-heaved. Bare beyond recognition, I put my hand on my forehead and nervously drew my thumb and middle finger across my eyebrows.

"No, you didn't!" she insisted as she wept. "Why don't you say it all the first time? This is a nightmare. I keep thinking you're saying everything, then you surprise me with more. Just tell me the whole story!"

I shut down, thinking: *What are we learning from this? Does this get us closer to closure? No! This is only causing more pain!*

Why do I continue daily face-to-face confession with the one I

4. Death To Self: Calamity

hurt?! She shouldn't have to bear this weight! How do I stay transparent without going too far? How do I stay sane? Am I sane to begin with? I hate this! Am I gaslighting myself? If I had a job, at least I'd be preoccupied. I wouldn't have time to be convicted of anything! I wouldn't have time to confess eighty percent of this garbage!

...Or would a job mean this process would stretch out five years? Ten years?

The kids entered the room, vying for attention. I turned to Ashley, defeated. "I guess we'll talk later." She left the room. I then turned to the kids. "I need to roast some chicken, then I'll come outside."

Our trampoline, a gift for Arlo on his fourth birthday, was used daily. An escape from monotony.

Arlo and I played *Red Light, Green Light*; a game called *Silence!* where Arlo and I would land in front of each other, seeing who would fall first; a game called *Poison Ball* where we rolled a small ball around the perimeter and tried to avoid letting it touch us; a game called *Helmets On!* where we'd proceed to chase a small ball, tripping and wrestling all the way; a game of me rolling from one side of the floor to the other, trying to knock Arlo over as he ran in circles; a game where my legs acted as a bridge crossing and Arlo would have to pay fifty cents to get through (when he didn't have enough imaginary money, he'd barrel through); and a game where we'd spray the trampoline with water, get in, declare "I will not slip!", then proceed to fall hard on the snare-drum surface.

But our absolute favorite was *David and Goliath* (or Golififf, as Eviana would say), during which Arlo and I would take turns as boy and beast. As Goliath, I would say, "Fee fi fo fum, I smell the bottom of an English boy." Then Arlo would say, "...an English daddy." Then we would swing our pretend slingshot, let go, and fall to the ground. Surrounded by cathartic laughter, I can still see Ashley holding Eviana as they watched us from the nursery window. Even with debilitating physical and emotional pain, she was trying.

As daily confession continued, I tore open old wounds, created fresh ones, yet felt relentlessly confronted by the Holy Spirit. I'd share two or three new confessions, ruining the rest of the day. Whether 8 a.m. or p.m., Ashley knew when I was holding on to something of importance. My face only read guilt and spoke sweat. She was desperate to know and desperate not to know. At the expense of her emotions, she wanted to understand me—whether the old or new. Her body language asked, *Why do so many of your sins seem to be sexual in nature?* She often knew when the next onslaught was coming. Her body was always rigid.

And sure enough, then came a new volatile confession of old, arbitrary sins, spanning years:

"I lied about who I was hanging with that day." *God, help me.*

"I wasn't ready to be married. I still don't understand what love is." *Lord, have mercy.*

"Yes, it was while we were dating." *Please make this end.*

"She cried to me about her husband." *Forgive me, Father.*

"I loved it when she sat next to me." *In Jesus' name. Amen.*

"I'm sorry." *I'm not cut out for this. What was I thinking? I ruined our vows.*

Then I heard the Holy Spirit whispering: *Rest, stay where you are, this is good.*

As I offloaded sins, Ashley hesitantly picked them up, folded, then placed them in her brain's bureau. One magnet was extracting sin shavings from me, while another drew them toward her.

4. Death To Self: Calamity

If my description of an incident was too vague, she was plagued by questions, insecurities, and fear of the unknown; if too descriptive, Ashley cried, haunted by despicable, involuntarily images; and if avoided entirely, our ice sheets drifted further apart.

As I handed boulders to Ashley, she reacted as expected; as I handed to her what I thought to be pebbles and clay, she often reacted unpredictably, also viewing these as boulders. Then it hit me: her perception was all that mattered, regardless of how it came to be.

Uncovering my disguise was detailed enough, but exposing every damn transgression I've ever committed transformed me into a Thailand cave-rescue SEAL. Among recesses, caverns, nooks, and crannies, were cavities, chambers, and deep pockets—each with its own infected lump of secrets. A suffocating atmosphere.

Yet, in the background, by God's grace, I whispered while shaking my head, *I'm reaping what I sowed. Father, if all of this is somehow right, keep it going. If it's not, please have it end. This is well beyond normal. People would laugh or cry at this, but I know your plans are bigger than anything. Please help us.*

5. EPIPHANY: A LOG IN THE EYE

The man said, "The woman whom thou gavest to be with me, she gave me fruit of the tree, and I ate."

—Genesis 3:12

I thought I had learned something. By now, nearly five months after my first confession, I thought I was selfless and calm despite the outrageousness of our journey. All the while resentment simmered within me, but I didn't know it—or maybe my pride wouldn't allow me to know it. Another façade, I suppose. My love and gratitude were still conditional. And what was the number one condition? Sex, or lack thereof.

After having been apart for quite some time, I was empty in every emotional category. On the couch, after a short conversation about a miscommunication, I abruptly screamed, "You're going to give me a heart attack!"

Naively, I thought we had cleared the sex hurdle after our marriage retreat. With betrayal at the forefront, I should've known it wouldn't be one hurdle, but a series of hurdles.

And a high jump.
And a long jump.
All at the same time.

Thank God the kids were down for their naps, both running white noise in their rooms. It was 2 p.m., and I hadn't gone for my afternoon walk. It was often the best medicine for frustration—sexual or otherwise. Predictably, my stubbornness kept me in a futile conversation.

"I try, I try so hard, then the smallest thing causes you to run," I added.

Ashley responded, "You're not listening to me. You're so caught up in your head. You're spinning your wheels because you don't understand me, or you don't know how to access your heart. It feels like you're checking boxes, but not understanding what the boxes mean."

"This is ridiculous. You're so complicated. You expect perfection," I retorted.

"I don't! I just want to feel loved," Ashley said with tears in her eyes.

"So do I!" I screamed again, ripping my hat off in a rage.

I then collapsed in the den in a heap of tears. I was glad all the shades were up. Light poured into the house. Dark rooms would've prolonged such strong feelings. Ashley stayed in the living room, likely outraged. As I curled on the floor like a toddler, I realized this episode was the latest chapter in a seemingly never-ending story of setbacks. Humiliated, I stayed there, trying to grasp the extent of what had just happened. *Why did I blow a fuse? Why that specific fuse?* The easy answer was lack of sex, but it was much more than that. I knew how to deny myself. I could choose to operate in flesh or spirit. *But how? How?! Why is she doing this to me?! This is not a game!*

5. Epiphany: A Log In The Eye

Original Cynicism

Just like sin itself, blaming is first traced to Adam. It only took a few verses to leap from *the fall* to *the finger pointing.*

Genesis 3 captures mankind's willingness to defer responsibility. In summary, Adam was given a specific command; it is inferred Adam relayed the command to Eve ("And the Lord God commanded the man"); Eve was confronted by the serpent; it is inferred Adam stood at her side ("who was with her"); Eve first ate of the forbidden fruit, then easily convinced Adam to do the same; God confronted Adam; Adam blamed God and Eve for his failure; God then confronted Eve; Eve blamed the enemy.

Adam was responsible from the beginning—literally. Even though Eve was deceived first and was rightfully reprimanded, God first challenged Adam. As it is recorded in Romans 5:14: "Yet death reigned from Adam to Moses, even over those whose sins were not like the transgression of Adam, who was a type of the one who was to come."

Drowning in shame, Adam blamed Eve ("the *woman*"), then God ("thou gavest"), declaring zero personal culpability. It seems this was Adam's way of deducing the following: 1) If Eve had not handed the fruit to me, I would not have eaten, and would therefore have remained in right standing with God; 2) If God had not given me a wife, I would not have had a hand from which to grab the fruit, and would therefore not have eaten, thus remaining in right standing with God.

Yet, in Genesis 2:23, Adam celebrated the fact he was given a wife: "The man said: 'This at last is bone of my bones and flesh of my flesh; she shall be called Woman, because she was taken out of Man.'"

Once sin entered the world, Adam's exuberance for Eve died. At the threshold of responsibility, it was easier to amplify the splinter in Eve's eye, and worse, impossibly, in God's eye. He threw Eve under the shrub in an effort to make a covering for himself.

As Adam, I celebrated Ashley, then blamed her; I marveled at her, then tolerated her; I committed to her, then committed to anything but her; I found a few faults, then I found all faults.

Similarly, with Genesis 3 as my compass, I could shamelessly seek a scapegoat, thereby becoming a new and improved scapegoat in the process—a tremendous excuse for rebellion to hand my children. If I blindly blamed others and my innate problems, I'd be forced to go to my parents, then beyond my parents, then beyond their parents and their parents' parents. Eventually, I'd reach the origin of sin, with the pointlessness of accusation right next to it. I might as well blame everyone for everything. Or I can be like Adam and "only" blame God and Ashley, or I can be like Eve and blame the enemy. Or I can blame no one, deciding to entrust myself to God and own my errors—regardless of how, when, why, and where the sin developed. "You are not your own; you were bought with a price. So glorify God in your body" (1 Corinthians 6:19-20).

It's simple to at least partially hold someone responsible for my faults—especially the most embarrassing. This cycle was nearly impossible to disrupt, much like every other sin I've described. However, when led by the Spirit, it became increasingly possible. As I took the focus off myself, I began to see others. As I saw others, I understood their shortcomings through the lens of my own. This did not render accountability meaningless and all behavior justified; it meant personal responsibility was now a priority. As in Matthew 7:4-5, "Or how can you say to your brother, 'Let me take the speck out of your eye,' when there is the log in your own eye? You hypocrite, first take the log out of your own eye, and then you will see clearly to take the speck out of your brother's eye."

5. Epiphany: A Log In The Eye

Without recognizing myself as a career sinner, I could not step out of myself. If it wasn't family, friends, or society to blame for my Rolodex of sins, it was Ashley for its continuation. Due to my perceptions of experiences, I could always claim victimhood in some capacity. Regardless of my childhood, race, gender, professed creed, or socioeconomic class, my feelings and my convenient interpretation of circumstances would win—every time.

I humbly returned to the Bible's teaching on sanctification, confirming special conditions did not exist. I can't imagine a verse stating, "...unless you're a victim. If you're a victim, some or none of these commands apply. In fact, you can do whatever you feel is right according to your will and life experience. After all, it's about what others have done *to* you, not what God has done *for* you."

This thinking is vanity and a striving after wind.

Empty Empathy

While unending confession incinerated my flesh (the "old man", according to Saint Paul), its ugly, selfish desires shouted, *You're doing fine. Ashley certainly has her share of mistakes; you're the one dealing with the real nausea. She has no idea what you're feeling.*

As a result, I struggled to consider Ashley's agony. Not glance at it, but honestly stare. It was possible at the marriage retreat, but that's because I was guided by a counselor. Otherwise, I was inept at accessing that part of my heart. I couldn't fathom crossing to—and remaining on—her side; pain framed a moat around my crumbling castle. Regardless, I continued to applaud myself for not regularly exploding with rage.

This restraint assured me that I was the bigger person, even while my confessions shaved inches off me. I was always fixated on *what caused the sin*, not *how the sin would impact Ashley*. I often rested between willpower and dead empathy, accomplishing nothing in the process. I exhausted all energy trying to confess and listen. To transition from listening to understanding felt unreasonable. The devastating breadth and depth of confessions had undermined my compassion. I thought, *Haven't we been here before?*

Admittedly, *she* was the bigger person—listening to my admissions, staying composed, then sharing her feelings while remaining calm as I gave blank stares, tired apologies, and half-stories. And since my façade had buckled, she knew when anything was awry, even fractionally. She knew when I was sinking in absent-mindedness, overthought, torment, guilt, or denial.

"What is it?"

"I feel like you're holding back."

"You might as well say the whole thing."

"Go ahead. I know you have something."

Should I say it? Should I shut up? Why won't this stop gnawing at me? I think I should say something. No—that's stupid. But when I do, it seems its power over me is broken. No—that's a trap, too, right? Then Ashley would have to carry the burden. That's ridiculous. Help me, Father.

"Why don't you just say what you're feeling?"

"Why do you let it get so far beyond your limit?"

"Just let me know, and we can take a break."

"If you share your thoughts when you're still calm, we can avoid a lot of this."

"I don't feel like you're empathizing at all. You completely invalidated my feelings."

5. Epiphany: A Log In The Eye

I thought, *Wait, we are not the same person. How am I supposed to feel empathy at her level? Heck, I'm out of empathy. Too many sins. Invalidate? How do I validate when I don't agree? Don't all men struggle with this? Maybe I'm trying to be someone I'm not. Or maybe this is just another challenge that requires sacrifice? Who is supposed to help a woman through her emotions? Who helps men? Dang, this is confusing.*

I turned to Scripture and was reminded to avoid harshness, which was only possible when mindful of Ashley's good attributes, not her wrongdoings. Critique persisted unless I gave thanks in all circumstances (1 Thessalonians 5:18), rejoiced with those who rejoiced, wept with those who wept (Romans 12:15), and bore one another's burdens (Galatians 6:2).

Is this right, or am I using Ashley's emotions to frame my theology? I need to keep exploring.

■ ■ ■

I recall Ashley expressing trust-building actions. They involved clear communication, sharing emotions while staying controlled, giving affection without wanting something in return (e.g. non-sexual hugging), providing protection, and using affirming words. To a still resentful and selfish man, this was a laundry list—the *law*, if you will. Surprisingly, in the middle of such "legalism," Ashley approached me with hope.

"You're starting to get me," she said, with full assurance. I don't remember where we were, but I snapped out of my months-long daze, if only for a moment.

"What?" I asked.

"I can tell you're trying to understand my feelings and I really appreciate it."

"Thanks for saying that," I responded. "I'm just trying to get past some stupid mental blocks. It's hard to explain."

But, like any seasoned victim, her complimentary words

shot out of my ears, and I returned to her laundry list with pessimism, reciting all the "chores" I had to do, all the "rules" I had to follow.

Then, to preserve some sense of equality, I replayed Ashley's needs, contemplating, *If living by the flesh, this is impossible; if living by the Spirit, however, could this be achievable, and even joyful?*

Suddenly, I was struck with optimism: only I know my thoughts and needs, AND I want them to be seen as valid as I see them, so why wouldn't her thoughts and needs be just as valid as mine? Even though the polar opposite of mine, that shouldn't render them dumb, made up, trivial, or dramatic. They are simply her needs. I then pondered something that significantly helped my mindset: *What if Ashley were terminally ill? How would I treat her? What would become of my needs? What if spiritually terminally ill? Emotionally terminally ill? How would I view her?*

Now when I confessed, I needed to simultaneously grasp Ashley's feelings. If she started to verbally attack—which was shockingly rare—I tried to listen and defer my strong reflexes to prayer time. I'd hear the Holy Spirit whispering: *She's right* or *Let her talk*. I didn't understand how seemingly small actions could have such significant impact on her, but it didn't matter. She needed to grieve.

I ignored the enemy's whispers of, *Yeah, but you wouldn't have done any of this if she was more _____, why are you resisting something natural anyway? This is a lost cause.* I strangled instincts and lies—they were of no help. I admitted mistakes without waiting for Ashley to comfort me, also knowing she had not committed similar sins and could therefore not reciprocate in solidarity.

Then I didn't. I hit a wall, expecting her to mimic me, expecting God to convict her of inexhaustible secrets. I asked myself, *Why doesn't she have the same issues I have? Why are her sins so different? She remains sinful outwardly. I am still leaning inward.*

5. Epiphany: A Log In The Eye

Because of my *shelf life* (the amount of time my virtues remained genuine), gentleness and kindness would suddenly expire—from good to bad in an instant. Just beyond this boundary were the emotional outbursts I could not afford. In these moments, I refused to see beyond poor ol' Eddie. Ashley knew of her shortcomings and was actively addressing them, but I was set on reminding her while adding typical, overexaggerated, juvenile fuel.

"You didn't respect me at all!" I yelled. "You didn't appreciate anything I did. You spoke to me like a child!"

Ashley looked away, muttering, "I did respect you."

I continued with other offenses: "You promised certain errands would get done, then you'd completely forget or ignore, as if you didn't care. It wouldn't even come up again until I'd finally say something days later. And that still happens! Your words mean less and less."

From this, I implied we must be experiencing the same emotions—mine through rejection and disrespect, hers through betrayal. Myopia at its finest. By forcing a parallel, I believed she should've been "over it" much quicker.

Even though this type of outburst often led to an apology from Ashley, these missteps were always damaging. Because I was still a geyser, fueled by an inability to understand her, I continued bringing up the past as a distraction. Even though the feelings were real, I was opposing my own realizations about women's needs, resentfully shoehorning into Ashley's sneakers.

I don't think I understand empathy. This is too hard.

Back to the drawing board. Thankfully, for the first time in my life, the board was God and not addiction. I cried out and He lifted me up. I inevitably returned to the Bible—often reading Luke, Galatians, or Ephesians—and attended to Ashley, even with my tail fused between my legs.

Choosing to love, regardless of circumstances and without

expectation of reward, is difficulty's apex. *Should my love not be predicated on a good response from her or her ability to meet my needs? Do I give only to receive, or do I give to give? Why does flesh always ask for something? Why so many pronounced, small cravings while large ones diminish?*

I didn't have an answer. And so it went. Lesson learned, misstep, lesson learned, misstep....

One afternoon as Ashley and I rested in bed during the kids' quiet time, her hopelessness was evident. As I scratched and clawed for details (knowing full well she had something monumental to share), she finally described herself as terribly broken, like a caged, abused animal who—as she cautiously approached an opening in the cage—was impatiently yanked out. She was then harshly reprimanded, causing her to recoil in her cage out of terror. She had become institutionalized. Each outburst caused her to retreat to the furthest part of the cage. My presence began to equate to tremendous pressure.

I realized that due to my unrealistic, roller-coaster expectations, I had caused Ashley to remain on edge. Whether it was purposeful or not was inconsequential. Because of my common responses to her insecurities regarding sexuality and vulnerability, she fearfully kept quiet. She sure as hell was not going to voluntarily bring up such issues again. She settled for walking on eggshells, awaiting my next spontaneous combustion.

Now in one of her lowest moments, I left the room so she could pray. I returned as soon as she was done.

"How did it go?" I asked.

"I believe the Holy Spirit showed me something. It was about you," she responded. "I was praying and asking God to show me how I'm going to get through this. When am I going to get past this? When will things not be so hard? Then, in my mind's eye, I saw you. I was watching you climb a mountain. You were hiking

5. Epiphany: A Log In The Eye

up a narrow crest line. I saw you reach the peak, plant your feet, rest your hands on your hips, and look out at everything below, just taking it all in."

"That's great, sweetie," I said, exhausted.

Ashley continued, "Then I asked God, 'Where am *I*? When will *I* get there?'"

With tears in her eyes, she turned to me with a Mona Lisa smile and said, "Your victory is my victory."

6. DEATH TO SELF: CAPTIVITY

There's a cross at the very center of human life. No man is ever really happy on the inside until he's at war with himself. At war with that which is base, and which would destroy his Godward tendencies. As our Lord said, "I came not to bring peace, but the sword." Not the sword that points and thrusts outward to destroy the neighbor, but the sword that thrusts inward in order to destroy one's egotism, and one's lust, and one's avarice, and all the things that destroy also a peace of mind. The greatest cross in the world is to be without a cross.

—Venerable Fulton Sheen

As I continued to fight daily, thoughts increasingly stalked and intimidated me. No matter what was achieved through Biblical application or epiphany, I was ceaselessly haunted by archived sins and traumas.

And the enemy sniper.

Miraculously, new weapons fell in my lap. Old verses

suddenly jumped out of the Bible and slapped me across the face, reminding me our madness would eventually come to an end.

- Romans 12:2 (emphasis added): "Do not be conformed to this world but be transformed by the *renewal of your mind*, that you may prove what is the will of God, what is good and acceptable and perfect."
- Ephesians 4:22-24 (emphasis added): "Put off your old nature which belongs to your former manner of life and is corrupt through deceitful lusts, and be *renewed in the spirit of your minds*, and put on the new nature, created after the likeness of God in true righteousness and holiness."

With this veil now lifted, I began to understand these Scriptures in light of my anguish. It equated to God's grace affording me an opportunity to do my part. Additionally, I was now acutely aware of sinful thoughts and was incessantly corrected.

Before this process, I expertly recited *Seinfeld* episodes and Norm Macdonald late-night talk show routines but couldn't recall Bible verses other than "Jesus wept" or "In all thy ways acknowledge him, and he shall direct thy paths." But now I needed to add to my stockpile of ammunition in order to "stand against the wiles of the devil" (Ephesians 6:11).

As I became aware of an abundance of my sinful thoughts and words—as well as what I had done and what I had failed to do—I finally comprehended 2 Corinthians 10:3-6 (emphasis added):

> For though we live in the world we are not carrying on a worldly war, for the weapons of our warfare are not worldly but have divine power to destroy strongholds. We destroy arguments and every proud obstacle to the knowledge

of God, and *take every thought captive to obey Christ*, being ready to punish every disobedience, when your obedience is complete.

Like the temptation of Jesus in Matthew 4:1-11, I needed Scripture to defend myself. Incredibly, I recalled Mike's parting advice from our last phone call to read Ephesians 6:17: "And take the helmet of salvation, and the sword of the Spirit, which is the word of God."

Grace Under Fire

When I hoarded offenses, refused to forgive, saw or heard filth, or rehearsed condemning words about myself, I dug trenches. As poor thoughts and decisions repeated for months, years, and decades, I effectively laminated and framed them, assuring commemoration. However, when compared to—and understood in light of—the Lord's commands, demolition began. Crowbars, sledgehammers, jackhammers, bulldozers, and explosives were delivered to the scene.

As I recognized or "caught" sinful thoughts, I prayed to the Lord to replace them with His goodness, or I recited Scripture, or I cried out in desperation, not knowing what I was saying and not caring how I sounded. Disgusting images poured into my conscience. At the worst moments, I rushed to my phone, typed *heaven* or *Jesus* into a Google image search, and stared at the results—for over a half hour at a time. I eventually settled on *Prince of Peace* by eight-year-old Akiane Kramarik. It was often the last thing I saw before closing my eyes for the night. It became my favorite replacement for the deceitful, wicked actors trying to occupy my brain.

■ ■ ■

Previously, at the thought of committing a sin, I halfheartedly or lazily resisted, yielding without a chance for escape. This was the easiest way to embrace cyclical transgressions.

For example, on my way to a networking wine event, I decided I wasn't going to drink. When I say "decided," it was like I had gently tapped a stake in the ground just once, then watched the first gust of wind remove it. I had gone a week without a drink and desired to continue.

At the door, however, I was greeted with a glass of Sauvignon Blanc. I didn't want to be rude, so I grabbed it. Within a few seconds, I found a table and placed it down, thinking, *Where's the water? If I'm not holding something, I'll look like an insecure freak.* As the event went on, high-schoolish peer pressure increased. By the third, "You're drinking water?", I caved. Internally, I blamed those who were giving me a hard time, but in reality, my lack of backbone and security—coupled with the temptation of alcohol—were the issues. Truthfully, I wanted an excuse: *This is some of the finest wine available. I can't turn it down forever.* By the end of such a night, I was a functional drunk. *See, you can handle it. How good was that wine?*

Such resistance isn't really resistance at all. It was this type which led to justified indulgence and slight remorse, if any. An episode such as this made the next much easier. What I internally labeled "backsliding" always became an advanced norm.

But now that my attempts were full-hearted, God was invited to the battle. His name was proclaimed at the onset. My initial thoughts, however innocent they appeared, were brought into captivity. As anger appeared, I recognized it. Not every time, but that didn't matter. I knew it was a layered process. If I was angry at Ashley, that was a starting point. When the thought entered, I repented and asked God to take the burden from me and

6. Death To Self: Captivity

replace it with fruit of the Spirit. Then I'd add, "I want nothing to do with it." As that form of anger lost power, another form of anger appeared, then I'd do the same. As I was doing that, a form of blame surfaced, then I'd do the same. Then envy, then the same. Then hate, then the same. Then laziness, then the same. Then jealousy, then the same. Then self-pity, then the same. Then depression, then the same. Any time I renounced these sins and feelings with repentance, God assisted me.

While some issues went away immediately, I fought others for months before their toxic trails were smothered (similarly, if no longer traversed, a hiking path will eventually be swallowed by nature). And as much as I hated this reality, I fought. There was no other way. I had to fight.

Ah, a moment of rest.

Then came overwhelming perverse, horrifying, infuriating thoughts. *What?! Why am I having these now? I'm trying to be pure, and I have to contend with new thoughts? I didn't have these before I confessed! What is going on? I've never thought like this in my life! This seems like a trap—a desert of quicksand. I HATE this!*

And just like that, my half-full glass became no glass whatsoever.

Then, like clockwork, involuntary renouncement kicked in. I was being trained. *What other choice do I have? I must get clean. God, help me.*

Then, back to pessimism and distress. Then rebuke. Then anxiety. Then more rebuke.

Stop. Go. Pennzoil.

■ ■ ■

I was so grateful to take captive old and new recollections of sin; distressing, fully-formed thoughts; and even peripheral thoughts—those which I could sense and stifle before they took shape. However, I knew their lifeblood was the ultimate goal.

I was so tired of reactivity. I knew if I was unable to assume a position of offense, the branches being cut would immediately grow back.

With God's grace, I was eager to rip out the entire tree, because even slow growth and dormancy were not options. Everything had to die.

I then realized many of my unwanted thoughts were originating not only from a poor view of others, but from what I saw and heard all around me. God made it clear how sensitive the eyes and ears can be. He revealed the little things that fester, grow, occupy, and infest.

Sadly, many trees seemed far out of my control. Trees which were stationed by the enemy. Trees which were trying to suffocate me.

Around this time, because I had nothing left to give, I disconnected from the majority of my friends. I wanted my old life to die since it was the very thing tormenting me day and night. Since I wasn't ready to confess the truth to others, I put on a new disguise. *I can't wait to be me*, I daydreamt. *I'm tired of playing parts.*

As friends and family called, I either provided pieces of the story (mostly tied to job searching) or ignored them altogether. Sick of distractions and interrogations, I changed my number, only updating a handful of people.

Ah, another moment of rest.

Then the purging continued. Ashley braced for impact as the Holy Spirit took over:

"I wanted her to notice me."

"When I was dressed well, I wanted all women to look at me."

"{Insert cuss word} entered my head occasionally. Divorce, too."

"I compared you to other wives. From our brief encounters, I assumed I knew how they treated their husbands."

6. Death To Self: Captivity

"The negativity and anger were overwhelming. I rarely controlled my thoughts."

"I was so blind, I acted like most of this was normal."

"I'm sorry."

Forgive me, Father, I whispered.

Then, as if to test my sincerity and integrity, the kids ran into the house, one of them knocking something off the coffee table. Enraged, I shouted without restraint. Even though I swallowed my pride and apologized later, the damage was done.

My comedic routine was concrete: hope, despair, hope, despair; hate, love, hate, love; faith, doubt, faith, doubt.

■ ■ ■

However microscopic, I was now aware of *every* thought. Thought captivity had become Eddie captivity. Now nearly deranged, I didn't want to think. When I did think, I desired to forget my thoughts. The very thought of forgetting thoughts meant I'd have to fight even harder. The very thought of not wanting to think meant I'd have to fight harder still.

Thankfully, no matter the sequence of measures, torture would eventually subside. However, it seemed my thoughts were being deferred—sometimes patiently, other times impatiently—to await me on the other end (e.g. when talking to Ashley, getting ready for bed, or when thinking, *Wow, it's been a good day so far*).

But again, somehow, training kicked in and pulled me up, forcing me to fight—every time. I was an underdog boxer wanting to give up and spare a concussion only to have my coach and cutman push me back into the ring as I resisted in a *Matrix* pose. Along with rejecting thoughts, I declared, *I am a son of God, I will not be shaken, I can do all things in Him who strengthens me. Blessed is He who comes in the name of the Lord. Hosanna in the highest!*

Anything to catch a breath.

My favorite verse became: "Rejoice always, pray constantly,

give thanks in all circumstances; for this is the will of God in Christ Jesus for you" (1 Thessalonians 5:16-18).

Around this time, I asked, *What exactly is His will? Do we have explicit direction in the Bible?* I found some verses, like 1 Thessalonians 4:3-7:

> For this is the will of God, your sanctification: that you abstain from unchastity; that each one of you know how to take a wife for himself in holiness and honor, not in the passion of lust like heathen who do not know God; that no man transgress, and wrong his brother in this matter, because the Lord is an avenger in all these things, as we solemnly forewarned you. For God has not called us for uncleanness, but in holiness.

I also recited 1 Corinthians 13:4-7, Ephesians 5:25-27, Romans 12:2, Job 31:1, Isaiah 53:7, Romans 5:3-5, Philippians 4:4-8, and James 5:11. All worked like shotgun blasts—some targeted, others haphazard.

Taking thoughts captive was like prying a large rock from the ground and exposing a village of bugs in their cool, moist homes.

This C.S. Lewis quote from *Mere Christianity* resonated with me:

> No man knows how bad he is till he has tried very hard to be good. A silly idea is current that good people do not know what temptation means. This is an obvious lie. Only those who try to resist temptation know how strong it is. After all, you find out the strength of the German army by fighting against it, not by giving in. You find out the strength of a wind by trying to walk against it, not by lying down. A man who gives in to temptation after five minutes simply does not know what it would have been like an hour later.

That is why bad people, in one sense, know very little about badness—they have lived a sheltered life by always giving in. We never find out the strength of the evil impulse inside us until we try to fight it.

Before first confessing to Ashley, whether it was alcohol, masturbation, or comfort food, I used to resist in intervals, then would not only cave, but binge. My sin loved to make up for lost time, rendering me a mouse in a sequence of wheels.

Thankfully, I was learning that even with better coping skills, strict willpower would never be the answer. Without collaborating with grace, I knew my "god" of addiction would persist.

Clearly, it was time for my god to be God Himself.

Once He was my top priority, I fervently guarded against replacements. Around this time, it struck me to take greater measures—those which many wouldn't understand, but were absolutely necessary for a guy who stretched inches to miles. My old habits did not and could not bring freedom; I had been trading pride for sexual immorality, anger for drunkenness, and shame for social media. But, by exchanging vice for virtue, I could stop medicating. So, while observing some of my remaining "drugs", I deleted Facebook and Instagram. If I had continued to cling to these platforms—even mildly—in lieu of severing them, it would have been like downing two Irish Car Bombs instead of six.

Admittedly, going cold turkey without a change of heart (Colossians 2:23) could easily promote legalism instead of sanctification.

Martyr Numb

In the midst of it all, I found a compartment in my brain I called "resting in pain." Whether containing a thought, trigger, or source of anger, it turned an otherwise infuriating reality into solace. I believe my mind dashed to this box to avoid a psychotic break. In these moments, I wondered if Ashley was doing the same. If my mind could somehow associate such horrible—nearly comical—issues with rest (the type the Holy Spirit seemed to be encouraging), I'd at least maintain some rationality. But, of course, even in this state of "rest," I'd occasionally internally yell, *This isn't fair! I can't keep doing this!* And with a biased memory, all lapses occurred at the worst possible times. Yet, despite the volcano of frustration inside me, I'd hear, *Stay where you are* or *This is good.* These directives equated to yet again opening my mouth, confessing, or sitting back in prayer, regardless of how I felt.

In an effort to accept the unexplainable, I drew an analogy. A scene that happened all too often at our house in Napa: a bird, flying full speed, crashing into our living room window. Ashley was always the first outside. I'd slowly follow behind, assuming the bird died. Three times out of four we found it quiet and breathing slowly. A few hours later, it was gone. We liked to imagine it flew away and was not easy prey for a cat.

At times, I was the bird, only to fly away and crash into the same window a few hours later. Other times, I was the concerned couple checking on my psyche, making sure I had not lost my mind. And at times, I was the cat, viewing the bird as a bad thought that needed to be destroyed.

Resting in the middle of such chaos was inexplicable. Nausea persisted, yet God often tapped my shoulder, reminding me that somehow this would settle. He provided wisdom, whispering, *It's her feelings that matter now. Stay the course.*

But—on some random day, at some random time, in some random room—my words detonated: "Why did it seem like you wanted to be so close to me, but then you'd refuse me? If you knew something was off, why didn't you say more?! I told you we should've seen another counselor together years ago! Damn it!"

6. Death To Self: Captivity

As I caught my breath, I focused further inward, wondering with full curiosity, *How can a person feel desperately needed and terribly rejected at the same time?*

I was convinced this latest outburst returned us to the starting line. But like any egocentric human, I focused on how rarely I lost it on Ashley, childishly thinking, *Hey, I've been so good throughout this, can't you see I'm allowed to explode every so often?* But, somehow, in an effort to regroup and retain some humility, I often conceded internally, *But who cares what I think?*

In these seesaw moments I found myself in a nightmarish haze, trying to cut through it by reading to the kids. But I couldn't make the words jump off pages like Ashley could. She often stepped out of herself to ensure they felt somewhat normal. I just sat and muttered line after line, completely clueless to the theme of the book.

The kids didn't leave, surprisingly. I'm assuming the colorful pictures were enough to maintain their interest. I was so happy to have them next to me.

Then, of course—on another random day, at some random time, in some random room—more spillage from the past followed:

"I took a narcotic I got from a coworker. I had a ton of joint pain. I thought it would help. It was when I had the week off and you were at work."

"I smoked weed and took shots with some buddies that day. It was only a little."

"A few months into dating, there was a girl at a company retreat. I'm not sure what we did. I almost blacked out, but I know for sure we didn't have sex."

"I ate some weird cookies from a friend of a friend, knowing full well they were loaded with weed. They must have been laced with something else though. I thought I was going to die. I was paralyzed for over an hour."

"Yep, we counted shots. I was up to thirteen or fourteen when I blacked out...I think."

Then, even while knowing my heart and mind were radically changing, an internal five-year-old tantrum exploded within me: *I didn't ask for this. I hate this process! This has to be a test. It has to be.*

Process of Humiliation

By now, I knew most admissions of guilt caused Ashley grief. I desperately wanted subsequent confessions received by her to elicit responses like, *Oh, no problem. You've already said things like that. That's totally fine.* Instead, her face read, *No matter how many things you say, small or large, they hurt me. This is cumulative, not a perpetual restart. I'm not choosing this. Even as I forgive, it just hurts.*

If I confessed, it stifled trust and intimacy; if I avoided, I felt disobedient toward God. And even though excruciating, I ultimately obeyed—often with prefaces that lasted minutes, hesitations that expended me, and excuses and emotions that manifested in thoughts like, *I'm not flawless! This makes zero sense. Why isn't God calling Ashley to confess fifty million thoughts and actions? If I hadn't played such a strong leading role as Mr. Perfect, would these sins have hurt her as much? If I had been just a little more genuine over the years, would this process be over?*

I now started any series of confessions with exaggerated cowardice and protective mechanisms, stuttering:

"This is so small, it's not a big thing...you know me. I don't think it's a big deal. It's just gnawing at me, so I guess I should say it...." And then, "So, I was thinking, yeah, I was thinking. Well, um, yeah, um, I'm only saying this because I feel prompted. It's not a problem, that's for sure."

"Just say it," Ashley would respond.

Whether in light or dark, in the living room or bedroom, on

6. Death To Self: Captivity

the couch or in dining chairs, it didn't matter. My confessional had visited every setting. There were no safe havens, it felt. All had given way to honesty. Deep, hated, insane honesty:

"Yes, I was attracted to her...and her...and her. Yep, even her. Whether they were a stranger or not was irrelevant. Weight didn't matter either. And it didn't matter if they were 25 or 55."

"I was strangely attracted to certain voices, too. Singers, actresses, you name it."

"Yes, I flirted with her...and her...and her."

"Temptation isn't even a sin! I don't even know why I'm encouraged to share this with you!"

"Rather than naming names, just know if you think I could've been attracted, chances are I was."

"When I say attracted, I'm not saying I wanted to have sex or anything," I said confidently during one confession. This installment took place in the middle of the afternoon in our living room.

"Well, what do you mean?"

"I thought they were good looking."

"Then why don't you say that? Noticing that someone is good looking is normal. But when you say 'attractive,' I tend to associate it with something sexual. Don't you?"

As I shook my head, I said, "I don't know. Obviously, I did scan many of those women, so I guess that goes beyond thinking they're 'good looking.' I just don't know. This is like us debating glancing versus staring. I'm so sick of this. I feel like I'm in a cage."

Ashley shook her head in return. "You think *I* want this? I'm just trying to understand you. I don't fully know what you battled and what you still battle," she responded. "By the way, I'm not controlling you. I'm not forcing anything. You're the one being told to share!" She quickly turned away, now staring at our living room rug. It was patterned with many imperfections, offering hours of entertainment during arguments. Our coffee table was far less exciting for drifting eyes.

"I viewed hundreds of women this way. Pornography made things much worse. It distorts them. Random women appeared in my head while I mastur....," I trailed off in disgust.

"I'd say that is well beyond thinking someone is 'good looking,'" Ashley said with equal disgust. "How is that not sexual?"

I wasn't sure what her posture meant, but she clearly did not want to be there. I was amazed by how rarely she walked out, however. She always stayed in one spot, awaiting resolution, regardless of how long it took. This time, however, I wasn't sure there'd be one.

I wondered if it was truly God permitting such craziness to play out—and if so, WHY?! Then I wondered if plumbing such depths was helping me understand the weight of Jesus' words equating lust to adultery.

Then, I retreated in a fit, asking, *What good is this serving? I don't know exactly what I felt! Is this uncovering some deep mystery? No! This is a nightmare. Seriously.*

Then a whisper from the Holy Spirit: *Keep going.*

■ ■ ■

In the grand scheme, the majority of what I confessed was insignificant to *me*. As these "pointless" sins entered my head, I began a process of denial, burial, and/or forced forgetfulness. I either dismissed the memory; sought to acknowledge it, then shoved it into oblivion; or mentally sprinted from it. However, because it seemed to be God's plan, ten times out of ten, I could not outrun, outsmart, or outthink these convictions. Therefore, I just needed to remain obedient in the best way I knew how.

In hindsight, this prayer from Thomas Merton's *Thoughts in Solitude* is fitting:

6. Death To Self: Captivity

> My Lord God, I have no idea where I am going. I do not see the road ahead of me. I cannot know for certain where it will end. Nor do I really know myself, and the fact that I think that I am following your will does not mean that I am actually doing so. But I believe that the desire to please you does, in fact, please you.
> And I hope I have that desire in all that I am doing. I hope that I will never do anything apart from that desire. And I know that if I do this you will lead me by the right road, though I may know nothing about it.
> Therefore will I trust you always, though I may seem to be lost and in the shadow of death. I will not fear, for you are ever with me, and you will never leave me to face my perils alone.

As I often did, I sat, shaking my head, thinking, *I can't fully describe to others how any of this feels, so they'll either trust me or label me psychotic. Regardless, the convictions are just too strong! I know when it's God!* But then someone will ask, "How do you know it's God? And how do you know it's the God of Christianity? Have you met Him?"

Bless Me, Father

Because of the strain my past was putting on the marriage, it was heartbreakingly tough to be intimate. And when not intimate, I was tempted, as warned against in 1 Corinthians 5: "Do not deprive each other except perhaps by mutual consent and for a time, so that you may devote yourselves to prayer. Then come together again so that Satan will not tempt you because of your lack of self-control."

However, even when intimate, I was tempted by clothing. At the grocery store, the gas station, the thrift store, the crosswalk, the doctor's office—all environments had the potential to erode endurance. I wanted to hide in a cave, but I knew the only solution was to fight through the very wasteland I couldn't understand or define.

Once tempted, I had several choices: I could give in and look, resist by the skin of my teeth (which meant the next time I'd look), or resist with such confidence that future temptations would weaken. Also, in what felt like another dimension, I found an occasional, puzzling "choice": unconsciously checking out women. I was always quick to tell myself, *There's no way that was lust! It was completely involuntary!*

Sadly, another nightmare had formed: virtually everything had the potential of becoming a sin in my mind.

As I struggled to understand the weight of even my smallest actions, and the possibility of losing my mind and going too far into legalism, Romans 7:21-25 came to mind:

> So I find it to be a law that when I want to do right, evil lies close at hand. For I delight in the law of God, in my inmost self, but I see in my members another law at war with the law of my mind and making me captive to the law of sin which dwells in my members. Wretched man that I am! Who will deliver me from this body of death? Thanks be to God through Jesus Christ our Lord! So then, I of myself serve the law of God with my mind, but with my flesh I serve the law of sin.

In the middle of these present temptations, I was struck with other issues of my past. Again convicted with an unimaginable fire to confess, whether regarding old girlfriends or habits of lying, I shared it all. I conceded it was helping Ashley better understand me, but I was only sharing because I thought I was asked to. The last thing I wanted to do was divulge new stories—specifically

6. Death To Self: Captivity

those which had not occurred when we were together. *How can this help anything? WHY am I being asked to do this?*

They all carried unpredictable weight. I staved off insanity by concluding that my life's painting was transforming from an abstract charade to a naturalistic portrait before Ashley's eyes. *This must be what God wants!* When my confessions were limited to our time together, which represented about one third of my life, Ashley's microscope viewed me with a 10x lens, then a 40x, then a 100x. As we explored the other two thirds of my life, we reached 400x and beyond. Once these old sins were spoken, I knew the coming hours and days needed injections of prayer. Amazingly, however, Ashley was calm and used sound reasoning ninety-five percent of the time. Regardless, I felt her curiosity and resulting pain were adding weight to confession.

"Why does it seem you need to know everything?" I asked.

"I don't! You keep talking—or your body language keeps talking," Ashley responded.

"Yeah, but it seems like you can't just say, 'It's okay. You don't need to mention every sin you've ever committed...every woman you've ever looked at,'" I continued. "This has clearly gotten out of control."

"As I've said many times, if you don't feel prompted to share, then don't," she said. "If it seems like I'm bugging you with questions, it's because I can tell something is weighing on you. You get so distant. Your guilt—or whatever it is—takes over. I can see it all over you. It's so obvious, and it makes me feel very insecure—like I'm walking through a minefield, waiting for an explosion. When I feel insecure, I pull away as well. We can't afford to add to the distance between us. If keeping these things to yourself causes so much torment for you, I'd rather you just say it. At least then I know what's going on, and we can work through it together."

"A lot of times...it's just hard to explain. I get attacked. I wrestle. I purge. I resist. The things I 'need' to confess rise to the top, regardless of what I do to escape them," I concluded. "Most of these 'sins' don't feel like sins in the first place!"

Most mornings I'd awake repressing memories, running from dreams I'd had that night. Sprinting from thoughts is indescribable. At my lowest, I begged for amnesia. If I saw too much skin in public—or while recalling a dream—I nearly broke into a sweat, mentally wrestling: *Do I need to confess that? No! God, there's no way that was a sin. There's no way! But I guess that doesn't matter anyway. I've been confessing temptations, too. No, it doesn't need to be said. This is another trap. This is so ridiculous!*

In the Second Note of his *Spiritual Exercises*, regarding persuasions of the enemy, Saint Ignatius of Loyola writes:

> ...or after I have thought or said or done some other thing, there comes to me a thought from without that I have sinned, and on the other hand it appears to me that I have not sinned; still I feel disturbance in this; that is to say, in as much as I doubt and in as much as I do not doubt. That is a real scruple and temptation which the enemy sets.

And in his Fourth Note:

> The enemy looks much if a soul is gross or delicate, and if it is delicate, he tries to make it more delicate in the extreme, to disturb and embarrass it more. For instance, if he sees that a soul does not consent to [...] any appearance of deliberate sin, then the enemy, when he cannot make it fall into a thing that appears sin, aims at making it make out sin where there is not sin, as in a word or very small thought.

6. Death To Self: Captivity

But I didn't know this. Even if I had, I doubt the train would've stopped. My convictions were too strong.

Trying to remain upright made me sick. I felt I needed to be perfectly pure, knowing full well how ludicrous it sounded. However, this wasn't a man trying to observe the entire Mosaic Law. This was a man just trying to remain chaste and devoid of any filth. *Am I obeying or have I somehow forced this on myself?* This—coupled with a hundred ups and downs in communication and intimacy—was unbearable. One step forward, one step left. One step backward, one step right.

Still—even in these despairing moments—I'd receive yet another conviction to confess old sins, further escalating the entire process. As it gnawed at me, I'd push it aside time and time again (*I need a distraction; I need to stay busy*), burying it with a series of songs, shooting hoops, then cleaning dishes, sweeping outside, taking out the trash, then eating lunch and dinner. *God, I should confess? No? What? Am I talking to myself? No, that was God. No, that was my own thought. What do you think God wants? More secrecy? At what cost?* Finally, I obeyed (or gave in, as it often felt), pulled Ashley aside, looked into her eyes, and prepared to pry my mouth open, as if to say, *It has been six hours since my last confession. These are more sins*:

"I saw them all on social media. It was everywhere. I could look up anyone's pictures—friends, coworkers, strangers. You name it. There really was no line."

"I stared. I lusted."

"I glanced at spam emails, knowing full well the content was sexually explicit. I don't know why—it felt involuntary."

"I had lunch with her—and drinks." *Everyone in the industry does this.*

"Just drinks with her. Yes, I paid."

"Yes, all those actresses. Every show we watched."

"My eyes were everywhere at once. They took in everything."

"I'm sorry."

Here comes that all-too-familiar repulsion crashing over me while Ashley sits and stares, likely thinking: *You can stop now. Please stop.* Once again, her emotions had peaked, but my latest episode managed to draw a few new expressions from her. If it weren't for a perfectly-timed, "I pooped!", from down the hall, you could've heard a pin drop.

I believe even a priest would've shouted, "That's enough, Eddie!"

I had become like Martin Luther during his own obsessive, scrupulous confessions.

In *Martin Luther: The Man Who Rediscovered God and Changed the World*, author Eric Metaxas writes:

> Once, Luther actually continued confessing for six consecutive hours, probing every nook and cranny of every conceivable sin and then every nook and cranny within each nook and cranny.
>
> [...] Luther seemed some kind of unprecedented moral madman on a never-ending treadmill of confession. Instead of looking upward and outward toward the God who loved him, he zealously and furiously fixated on himself and his own troubling thoughts. Johannes von Staupitz, [Luther's confessor], once said, "Look here. If you expect Christ to forgive you, come in with something to forgive—parricide, blasphemy, adultery—instead of all these peccadilloes.
>
> [...] [Staupitz] could see that Luther was chasing his own tail.

If only I knew then what I know now.

7. EPIPHANY: AS CHRIST LOVED THE CHURCH

Husbands, love your wives, as Christ loved the church and gave himself up for her, that he might sanctify her, having cleansed her by the washing of water with the word, that he might present the church to himself in splendor, without spot or wrinkle or any such thing, that she might be holy and without blemish. Even so husbands should love their wives as their own bodies. He who loves his wife loves himself.

—Ephesians 5:25-28

It had been a while since Ashley discovered she was pregnant with our third child, and since the moment she found out, we hadn't been intimate.

"This is garbage. You repeatedly did the same thing during our first eight years!" I said. As with so many disagreements, my issue related to the physical, while Ashley's related to the emotional.

"What do you mean?" Ashley asked.

"You played the *'How do you keep a moron in suspense? I'll tell you tomorrow'* game with me. If I blew a fuse because we hadn't had sex for an extended period of time, you would say, 'If only you could've seen how close I was to taking a step forward.' If I didn't blow a fuse, yet pursued sex, you'd say, 'If only you could wait for me.' This is nuts. It's a lose-lose mind game, and it has been for years." Because I didn't care how I sounded, I'm sure any therapist would've wanted such a discussion to happen in-person, with all three of us in a safe, cozy room.

I continued, "When you're pregnant, I feel even more rejected. This is stupid. I'm respecting our bed. I have never been cleaner, and my intentions are pure."

To the best of my knowledge, I thought.

Ashley paused with tears in her eyes. She saw the situation from my viewpoint. Her empathy hit the bullseye. "I understand now how the things I did affected you, and I'm sorry. I didn't feel safe, but I absolutely cared. I was paralyzed. It was all a disaster. I was just as hurt and confused as you were. I swear I was not trying to manipulate you. I hope you can see it's different this time," she responded. "However, with this pregnancy, it's a coincidence. Two days after I told you I was pregnant, we had a huge fight, don't you remember? Since then, we've been in another stupid cycle. Just like you, I'm not the same person I was before. We've got to find a way out."

Remaining on the edge of combustion, I left for a walk. I started with lead in my shoes and—without explanation—ended with helium. Unaware of God leading me to another lesson, I was drawn to Ephesians that evening. As I scanned chapter five, it jumped out of the Bible, assumed a karate stance, then knocked me out with a seven-hit combo.

The words *as Christ* were a jetliner.

As I looked up from the page with tears in my eyes, I knew another blindfold had fallen. I was now absorbing a decree which refused shortcuts, excuses, and conditions. This command represented a choice I was previously ignorant of—a non-negotiable

7. Epiphany: As Christ Loved The Church

sacrifice. A sacrifice available to me, regardless of circumstance. As I had learned Biblical commands—especially those instructing the treatment of my spouse—I found none that were conditional. None were malleable based on how I was treated, how Ashley responded, or what she was—or was not—doing. They remain unchanged regardless of the time of day, skewed Biblical interpretation, or a person's current mood. But I didn't know this. I didn't want to know this. I revered my vincible ignorance.

So, even with such a monumental epiphany, I got lost in thought, not knowing if my motive was love or fear: *Why are husbands called to love just as Christ? Why are some verses addressing husbands first while others address wives first? Should I assume wives should lead by example? Husbands? What if I have an epiphany first? Should I wait for Ashley to meet me before I act, or should I dive in according to what God has shown me?*

Confused, I kept studying.

Looking for a firm foundation, I now desired to understand unity of sexes. I soon found 1 Corinthians 11:11-12: "Nevertheless, in the Lord woman is not independent of man nor man of woman; for as woman was made from man, so man is now born of woman. And all things are from God." We are all from God *and* from one another. This plainly reinforces our subjection to God while also emphasizing men and women as equal sons and daughters.

I returned to my thoughts: *In marriage, what then becomes of equality? Where do we gain an understanding of the marriage model? How do husbands and wives actively participate? How does Christ relate to the Church? Husband to wife?*

To answer these, I asked more questions: *Did Christ first give Himself up for the Church, or did the Church first follow Him? Did Christ wait for the Church to do its part, or did He continue with His mission regardless? Did Christ abdicate His role out of apathy? For whom did Christ lay down His life? Did Christ lead by example or wait for someone else to take His place? Did Christ obey His Father because mankind was flawless?*

Not only did Christ act first, but His very actions are what saved the Church and displayed the height of obedience, submission, and leadership. And without such a standard, we'd forever leave each other, hopelessly seeking perfection. I also considered another portion of the equation: God did not create us to automatically love or hate Him. If He had, we would be computerized. If computerized, all would be meaningless: theism, atheism, sin, judgment, heaven, hell, work, play, love, hate, life itself.

When discussing free will, C. S. Lewis writes:

> Of course God knew what would happen if they used their freedom the wrong way: apparently He thought it worth the risk. Perhaps we feel inclined to disagree with Him. But there is a difficultly about disagreeing with God. He is the source from which all your reasoning power comes; you could not be right and He wrong any more than a stream can rise higher than its own source. When you are arguing against Him you are arguing against the very power that makes you able to argue at all: it is like cutting off the branch you are sitting on.

I choose to follow Him, to love Him. As a husband, it's no different. Love is an active choice, not a simple emotion that ebbs and flows based on needs being met. If I coerced or forced Ashley to submit to me, I'd be showcasing the inverse of Christ—and just the same if I insisted on ruling the household without acknowledging Ephesians 5:21 (emphasis added): "Submit to *one another* out of reverence for Christ." As I learned from RSV Bible commentary, "Even if such submission is not strictly identical, it is reciprocal and self-sacrificing."

However, when stubborn and prideful, I internally whined,

7. Epiphany: As Christ Loved The Church

Christ set an example for all humanity, not just men. Aren't I doing enough? I'm forgiving, refusing excuses, actively working on my issues, studying the Bible, praying, leading, spending time with the kids. Ashley should be doing her part alongside me (as subjective as that is). *She's not doing all the things I am!* (even though she was).

{Insert marital legalism}

I realized, however, by assuming I knew everything she was and was not doing, underlying tension swelled. Regardless, by then I was forced to ask, *Even if my idea of "her part" is forced upon her, what good does that do? Just imagine....* "HEY—YOU NEED TO BE LIKE CHRIST! (*While I get to be Judas!*)" *Yeah, that would work. And what would her part look like anyway? What is acceptable and unacceptable? When does Ashley finally pass the test? When is she good enough? And if she doesn't have the same marital epiphanies I have, does that mean I should coerce her under the guise of headship?*

Because this answer is so subjective, constant dissatisfaction is likely. It also creates a mentality where I contend for Ashley to move first, blind to my role. If I am busy observing what she lacks while ignoring or inflating my responsibilities, resentment will set in, as it did over the years. Furthermore, no wife can meet all Biblical commands, so it would serve me well to memorize and act out Philippians 4:8: "Finally, brethren, whatever is true, whatever is honorable, whatever is just, whatever is pure, whatever is lovely, whatever is gracious, if there is any excellence, if there is anything worthy of praise, think about these things." This mindset was crucial in reversing the toxicity of perfectionism.

Knowing full well Ashley was apprehensive, my responsibility did not change: lead and serve by surrendering to God. Nothing was to be achieved through sheer will, better debating skills, physical or verbal force, or cowardice and apathy.

I needed grace.

Of course, I knew lasting change required both of us—in

fact, it was the very thought I had to stifle. If I dwelled on Ashley's participation, I lost sight of mine. I realized, either before or after catastrophe strikes—regardless of who did what to the relationship—may the head lead the body.

Lease-To-Own Head & Body

As a Christian husband, I am appointed to a position of sacrifice: head of household. Whether obedient to God or not, this role persists. I can either assume or abdicate it, but I am the head, nonetheless. When I absorbed this reality, I was obligated to act on it. As indicated in Philippians 3:16: "Only let us hold true to what we have attained." In other words, as I read several verses on the role of a husband—and understood them—I became responsible for their truth. That's when it registered: sacrificial love is encouraged in any marriage; in Christian marriage, it is mandated.

Over the years, when I abdicated headship, I induced a coma. I remained intact with my *body* as indicated by "one flesh," but there was not an active brain occupying the cranium. The space was empty. Therefore, how could the *body* function properly?

In an attempt to fill the vacancy, Ashley sought to rent, if not own, the available space. This could manifest in many ways. She could assertively try to make me subject to her; remain or become passive, thus allowing a headship void to seem acceptable; seek to disengage from all males in an attempt to curl into victimhood; or mimic my God-given role, either acting content or resentful as the interim solution.

In our worst moments, Ashley had assumed a form of headship, speaking with frustration and dominance. She was probably angry about my fake sense of leadership, my false sense of loving. I must have thought my 9-to-5 job was all I needed to contribute to our marriage.

As she became one part head and one part body, I could

7. Epiphany: As Christ Loved The Church

either become passive and apathetic or aggressive and overbearing. I chose a majority of the former and a minority of the latter. As a mostly passive husband, I could: A) rest in no man's land, completely disengaged; B) resentfully assume the role of the body; or C) comfortably assume the role of the body. I chose option D) both A and B. Honestly, I was C at times as well. Clearly, another cowardly coping mechanism.

I checked out. Sure, I was still semi-present and productive. I went to work and out to dinner with family and friends, played a few pick-up games of basketball here and there, and spent many hours in front of the TV with Ashley. We stared and stared, awaiting bedtime. Our house was often a pigsty and our food choices were slop.

Ashley articulated her heartfelt emotions many times, but my ears were half-closed. The net result was stagnation. Even if my well-intentioned wheels were moving, we were sinking.

As a disgruntled husband, I started with one spousal issue, then quickly stacked offenses, which assured me that my ideals were unattainable. In this state, even when Ashley progressed towards my needs, nothing overrode my perception of the past. Her efforts and considerations were supposed to be sticks of dynamite to my mountain of hurts, blasting rock to make a tunnel. Instead, they were mostly duds. The result: bitterness. Often echoing in our household were her grumblings: "I feel like it's never enough," "I can't do anything right," "You're never satisfied."

I expected perfection of Ashley, while anticipating applause for every one of my efforts—even if such efforts had nothing to do with what she truly needed. Prideful even then.

All is vanity and a striving after wind.

Stiff-Necked People

Dr. Seuss' *The Zax* is one of his shortest—albeit densest—stories. It highlights two creatures: one who only walks west and another who only walks east. After a long distance, they eventually meet face-to-face, and rather than simply step to one side, they presumably stand in place for years, if not decades. Neither will budge in their stubbornness, so the world changes around them. Readers are to conclude they are arguing to this very day.

Reflecting on this story, I realized my marital rigidity. Cemented in pride, I always waited for Ashley to yield. My side was, *If only she would see my hurt; if only she could stop being so selfish; if only she would see my side; if only she would do her part.*

And since I only surrendered to myself, my thinking was always reasonable. While using Scripture as the basis of an argument, there was always a verse backing me up, even if totally out of context; likewise, Ashley. What comes first? A Proverbs 31 woman? An Ephesians 5:25 man? Each of us could have conveniently pulled out the Bible to encourage change or to justify why we weren't required to initiate anything—be it intimacy, conversation, apology, or forgiveness. It all depends on the lens.

"It is not the gospel you believe, but yourself."

The Bible is your oyster.

I can picture the following internal—if not external—dialogue between spouses.

Husband: "You should submit to my leadership."
Wife: "You should love me unconditionally."
Husband: "You should respect me."
Wife: "You should love me."
Husband: "Like Eve, you should be a helper."
Wife: "Like Adam, you should be a protector."

If living by the flesh, initiation of maturity is hell on earth. *Why would I want to say sorry again? I always say sorry. Why doesn't*

7. Epiphany: As Christ Loved The Church 119

she say sorry more often? Why should I be the first? She started it! Infantile.

Once this hurdle was visible and understood—even if partially—the goal was clear: set a standard of honesty and responsibility; be in connection with Ashley emotionally and spiritually; consider her deepest feelings and ambitions; and strive for heightened communication. However, my "manhood" and innate opposition to deep emotions did not want to concede for the sake of her any more than a Democrat or Republican wants to concede for the sake of the other.

Still, I humbly acknowledged my design to carry a greater weight, to shoulder a greater responsibility—to deny myself physically and emotionally for the sake of Ashley. Still, I tried to argue with God on this matter, but I had nothing to back me up—just empty interpretations and a last-ditch, *Yeah, but....*

If acting as a leader, I was to follow Christ and not worry about the impact on my pride, ego, or friends' perceptions. And not worry I was somehow weak to the rest of the world. And not be concerned about giving Ashley the dreaded "upper hand." And not worry about how the game is played. And not worry about how others could view it as humiliating or emasculating. The only item on my list was to pick up the cross in front of me. Whether a small or large issue, I was to lead.

As an example: I realized Ashley hadn't hugged or kissed me in days. (*Or had I not hugged and kissed her in days?*) Did I:

- A. get upset and confront her,
- B. assume she didn't care and begin harboring resentment,
- C. gently bring it up,
- D. or go up to her, kiss her, then give her a hug?

As petty as it sounds, in our strained marriage, this type of scenario was all too common. In the past, A and B were no-brainers—practically reflexes. Transitioning from those to C and D was like pulling tusks from a walrus. However, God's grace made it possible. I wanted to embrace rejection and self-pity, yet I was learning to do what I expected of Ashley. She reciprocated. We began understanding the power of doing the opposite of our previous actions (often a sacrifice, regardless of its size).

But, like every other lesson learned, I knew mistakes would precede accomplishment.

8. DEATH TO SELF: AUTOIMMUNITY

> *Count it all joy, my brethren, when you meet various trials, for you know that the testing of your faith produces steadfastness. And let steadfastness have its full effect, that you may be perfect and complete, lacking in nothing.*
>
> —James 1:2-4

In the summer of 2016, a little over year before I confessed, Ashley's health declined. We were at Old Fisherman's Wharf in Monterey, having walked a quarter mile from the parking lot.

"Honey, I'm hurting. I need to rest," Ashley said.

"What happened?" I asked.

"I'm having trouble walking. I'm not sure what's going on," she responded.

"Should you call the doctor when we get home?" I asked. "How bad is it?"

"Not good."

Quick to find an interim solution—when we arrived home a

few days later—we did nothing. I think we believed it would simply go away. But, only days later, Ashley had a flare of unbearable pain.

She called me at work, crying, "Can you please come home? I can't even lift Eviana out of her crib."

Later that day, she made an appointment with a rheumatologist. An array of tests were promptly ordered.

Two weeks later, as Ashley drove home from her follow-up appointment, she hopelessly called, saying, "I have rheumatoid arthritis *and* lupus. She said autoimmune conditions tend to come in clusters."

I probably thought, *Well, now there will be even less sex.*

We then scrambled from specialist to specialist, from research article to online forum, from clear conclusions to muddled decisions. We fought to understand what would alleviate pain, but most importantly, the cause of it. A simple explanation of "You have extreme inflammation" was sufficient in the moment but certainly not the long term. While researching causes of inflammation, we reluctantly decided medication was our best short-term solution. In conjunction, we began altering our food habits. Less dairy, gluten, and sugar—but we still did not know what we were up against.

However, on we went. I joined Ashley not in solidarity, but in need myself. I had been dealing with digestive health issues for years at this point and—just like drinking alcohol to escape myself—I knew adding another drug to my arsenal would not address the core issue.

I'd like to believe this drew us closer together, but my selfishness wouldn't allow that. My lens of Ashley's shortcomings did not change because of her newfound conditions. I now ask myself, *What would it have taken? Would cancer have changed my* heart? Paralysis? A vegetative state? When would I have placed her needs above my own?

Rebellion won. It always won, even if incrementally.

Lethargy of the Hours

A year into our marriage, Ashley developed chronic, debilitating exhaustion. During the week, she arrived home an hour before me. Many times, I'd open the door and find her sound asleep. Unable to explain why she was so tired, she'd often cry, confused of the cause, always assuring me she was taking the correct dosage of thyroid medication.

On the weekends, she awoke before me, but was regularly asleep on the couch within a few hours. On one particular afternoon in our apartment, she nodded off as I worked on the computer. A half hour later, she awoke in a chilling panic.

"Why didn't you come over to help?!" she asked. "You didn't hear me?"

"No. I didn't hear anything. What are you talking about?"

"I woke up, but I couldn't move. There was this tremendous sense of evil. I couldn't see it, but I could feel it there. It was right there, hanging over me. I know it's crazy, but I swear I was awake! I could see you, but I couldn't talk or make any noise. I finally figured out I could change my breathing, so I started breathing faster. I thought the sound would make you realize something was wrong, and maybe come shake me or something."

Confused, we frantically searched for an answer. Quickly, we found *sleep paralysis*. I had never heard of such a thing.

"You need to see a doctor," I said. With visible fear, Ashley agreed.

Within a week, she was monitored overnight by a sleep specialist. Conclusion? Idiopathic hypersomnia.

A few years later, while pregnant with Arlo, her legs broke

out in a rash. The severe itching lasted for months, often leaving her in tears. While pregnant with Eviana, her temperature was elevated for over a month.

Regardless of severity, maladies were too common in the Trask household. I began questioning why so many issues were arising, knowing Ashley was not a hypochondriac. But me? According to Ashley, maybe a little. I can catch a Man Cold like nobody's business.

Ashley's medical cadence was erratic:

Blood test. Your levels are low. Up your dosage. Get more sleep. Blood test. Miscarriage. Blood test. You're stressed. Antidepressant. Endocrinologist. Rheumatologist. Dermatologist. Keratosis Pilaris. Blood test. Miscarriage. Blood test. Atopic eruption of pregnancy. RhoGAM shot. Blood test. TMJ.

Everything culminated in fatigue. Ashley was always chasing an extra hour of sleep, never to find it.

TMI

I believe my chronic digestive issues began in 2006. Grabbing a simple meal was a literal crapshoot. I ate Italian food. Diarrhea. Mexican food. Diarrhea. American food. Diarrhea. A deli sandwich. Sometimes fine. Sometimes diarrhea.

Perhaps the most embarrassing incident was in San Francisco. We had been married for two days and had just been rejected on our honeymoon flight to the Dominican Republic because I used Ashley's married name on the tickets (which did not match her passport). I found myself being hypnotized into signing up for a timeshare presentation just outside Pier 39's parking garage.

Not a bad start.

After such humiliation, I was looking to stuff my face. Once we found a lunch spot, I confidently ordered a Seafood Deluxe Platter, expecting only the freshest selection. An hour later, by

8. Death To Self: Autoimmunity

the time we returned to the parking garage, I felt I was either going to pass a kidney stone or vomit myself to death. Neither happened. Instead, I squatted between cars while Ashley checked for security guards and tourists. I'll never forget her balanced look of concern and amusement. Marriage is bliss.

The same happened a few years later. A quick stop for lunch in Walnut Creek, then straight to Napa to meet our real estate agent who had a special property to show us. Somehow we arrived at the house five minutes before him. I ran to the back yard, squatted in the nick of time, and pulled up my pants moments before we heard a car door closing.

The same happened a few years later. We were enjoying an outstanding dinner with four of our closest friends at an upscale Napa Valley restaurant. By the time dessert rolled around, I was in the bathroom in agony, disrupted by knocks on the single stall every few minutes. I came back to the table twenty minutes later without a word. My friends likely thought the worst but respectfully kept it to themselves. As Ashley and I headed home, stabbing abdominal pain took over. Ten minutes from the house, I bolted for the nearest parking lot, then rushed to the closest toilet. The stall wouldn't close, there wasn't an air freshener in sight, and the toilet was set so far back, I had to proceed with the door open.

Then there were times I knew the risk yet chose to partake anyway.

The time I ate carnitas tacos (with special sauce) from a taco truck in Hanford, California, in 110-degree weather; the time I ate a soggy clam and shrimp dish in Winona, Minnesota (the heart of seafood country); and the time I ate sweaty mozzarella on our honeymoon. Same result: shooting pain in the abdomen, followed by diarrhea. Highly predictable, yet my appetite overrode the off appearance of food and its obvious consequences. Too familiar.

For years I felt I couldn't win, so I accepted discomfort. I made thoughtless choices and reasoned away the results. Finally, I saw a doctor. Then another. Then another.

My medical cadence was erratic:

Blood test. Blood test. Gastroenterologist. General practitioner. Neurologist. Endoscopy. Colonoscopy. CT scan. Probiotics. Prebiotics. Anti-depressant. H. Pylori. Fibromyalgia. Arthritis. Inflamed gut lining. Alarming levels of harmful bacteria. Parasite. High cholesterol. Anxiety. Blood test. SIBO. Mast Cell Activation Syndrome.

I can still hear a chorus of doctors:

"There's no such thing as a leaky gut!"

"Any time I hear of more than eight symptoms, my patient is depressed."

"You need to lose weight."

"Here's a list of what you're not allergic to."

"You're borderline celiac."

"Here, take these sample pills. And here's a free branded pen and notepad in case you forget the name of the drug."

At Twilight You Shall Eat Flesh

Optimistically, we made slight changes based on simple Google searches. Add some broccoli, remove some sugar. Add some berries, remove some pesticides. Add some L-Glutamine, remove some GMOs. However, the further we dove, the more confused

8. Death To Self: Autoimmunity

we became. Much like Christian infighting, every other opinion appeared contradictory. I then scoured the internet for functional medicine doctors and practitioners in the area, having learned of their approach to inflammatory disease. We urgently needed someone to make sense of such a complex landscape.

Finally, by God's grace, I found Laura.

After being diagnosed with an autoimmune condition, Laura forged her own path to natural healing. She did the heavy lifting, hoping others would benefit from her trials and errors. Since simply medicating was not an option, the root of the problem needed to be addressed, which meant a painstaking, sacrificial process was necessary. Band-Aids were of no use.

Laura had been practicing for over a decade, worked with patients remotely, and had dealt extensively with both of our conditions. She immediately arranged a strict plan for us, involving a drastic change in food selection. Secondarily, exercise, supplements, and rest.

Even with Laura's help, we resisted absolute commitment for several months. Instead, we added bits and pieces of the program. Unsurprisingly, we remained in pain. Shaking off laziness and fear, I finally decided it was time to digest Laura's forty-page guide to healing the gut. I circled words and phrases I didn't understand, reduced the number of pages to my top ten, and created a mock menu. I then overlapped the menu with my known allergies to reach a comprehensive list of acceptable foods.

In April of 2017, five weeks after baptism and five months before confession, I adopted the AIP (autoimmune protocol) diet, which seeks to reduce overreactive inflammation in the body. The list was so exhaustive and restrictive, it was easier to explain what I *could* eat. The list of *could not* was long and depressing. I was reduced to vegetables, root starches, coconut, olives, avocados, clean meat sources, and some spices. That meant no grains, legumes, nuts or seeds, alcohol, coffee, nightshades (potatoes, tomatoes, peppers), sugar, and minimal fruit (if any) since I carried bacteria that fed on fructose.

This was supposed to be a short-term solution.

Humbly, I learned how much I took for granted, how much people disagreed with this approach, how much money it costs to eat well, how much discipline I lacked, how much frustration stems from adhering to a radical new lifestyle, and how much effort it takes to avoid masking symptoms with drugs.

Neither Ashley nor I knew how to cook much of anything. For the length of our marriage, we had eaten trash; our main food groups were processed carbohydrates, dairy, veggie meat products, and wine. Our bodies had been pummeled.

And so, April was brutal. The checklist was long: learn how to shop properly; learn how to cook properly; learn how to chew food (not inhale it); learn how to incorporate the AIP lifestyle in the ever-tempting, ever-gorging wine industry; learn how to restrain myself from grabbing snacks, caffeinated drinks, and alcohol; and learn how to help raise and have time for my children in the middle of it all.

A guinea pig for the first five weeks, I patiently waited for Ashley to mentally prepare for a paradigm shift.

The meat aspect of the diet was a massive problem for her, since she was a die-hard vegetarian. Raised Seventh Day Adventist, it's all she really knew. While she did have some minor exposure as a child, she opposed it for four reasons: taste, smell, texture, and cruelty. The trump card was her love of animals. She. Loves. Them. I respected this—a lot. However, at the risk of her own life, given the other approaches we had taken, AIP was a logical next step. And once my weight, food cravings, and some of my emergency digestive problems diminished, I saw Ashley's hope increasing.

Yet, as commencement day approached, I became annoyed. I thought I understood her apprehension, and by validating her

8. Death To Self: Autoimmunity

concerns, I assumed she would switch gears. But she didn't. Taking her first bite of chicken was overwhelming. The second bite wasn't much better. By the tenth bite, she was still working on the first bite. It didn't help when the person preparing the meat only had previous experience making hot dogs and hamburgers. I certainly didn't know how to sear halibut, roast turkey, or hunt bison.

But, as the months dragged on, it got easier at times.

Amazingly, Ashley and I were bonding through the difficulty. We were exhausted from life (and at the time, probably didn't understand why), yet pledged support for one another as we considered the possible redemptive aspect of the journey.

Then, a brick wall:

MY FIRST CONFESSION.

Time stood still as our food rotation idled. We were suddenly in a cage of the same four to five foods, slapping meals together at the last minute and simplifying the menu repeatedly as Ashley dropped to an unhealthy weight. Every subsequent round of confession made getting off the couch nearly hopeless, but we knew we needed complete meals. We could not afford to sabotage our progress.

In the middle of it all, Ashley visited her rheumatologist, fully expecting an additional medication to be prescribed. This time she suspected an immunosuppressant. However, instead, her doctor declared, "I'm not sure what you're doing, but whatever it is, keep doing it. It's working."

A flood light to our darkness, even if momentary.

Despite the utter disaster occurring in our house, I appreciated the fact that Ashley thanked me for every meal I made. However, as soon as such relief appeared, it was gone. Her face while taking a bite of salmon, having heard my strip club confession an hour earlier, was the height of unsettling.

While at the table as a family, we relied on the kids to joke around. Unbelievably, we laughed a lot. The kids were stand-up comics visiting a prison. Once we excused them from the table, we returned to our cyclone of insanity. We'd often look up to piles of glasses, pans, and utensils, wishing we had a dishwasher.

During the first nine months of AIP, I don't remember ever seeing Ashley cheat on the diet. She was a soldier. But me? Less than a week after I first confessed, I ate cheese, chocolate candy, and drank a cup of coffee, as negligible as that sounds. These decisions did not derail the plan—even though that wasn't the key issue. My dreaded *shelf life* had infiltrated every aspect of my life.

Any time we traveled, it was a sideshow. I'd cook as much food as possible beforehand. We'd stuff the food in our trunk, back seats, and even in Ashley's lap. The height of this juggling act was during our marriage retreat. Our hotel mini fridge was swelling with five days' worth of chicken, sweet potatoes, cauliflower, and cassava tortillas. We rationed down to the last wedge and floret. Friends and family took various positions on the matter. Some openly, some in secret, and some in between, acting their way through what appeared to be hell for them. "Wait, you can eat what?" "You can't eat what?" "You're allergic to what?!"

I didn't want to go anywhere with anyone. Ashley felt the same, but it had nothing to do with food. She was tired of acting her way through family visits; shattered inside, yet forcing a smile.

From *my* old façade to *our* new façade.

"Everyone thinks we're freaks, Ash," I said.

"No, I don't think so," she responded. "I don't think anyone thinks badly of us. I just think they don't fully understand."

I was surprised to hear her optimism.

"Regardless, I'm sick of this. I don't know what to eat, how to diversify, how to stop feeling sorry for myself. I just want this crap to end. Why can't we just be hermits? Can you imagine if they knew the whole story? They'd definitely think we're insane."

"I know what you're saying. But we're not freaks. We're doing what's right for us. Our issues are improving, right?"

"I guess so. I just hate feeling like we're so overwhelming to cook for, especially when I've made it clear I am not trying to force our issues on other people, but I guess that's impossible. We've offered to bring our own food. If I just eat whatever is served to me, I will have issues. Same with you. I hate feeling like we're a burden, but what else are we supposed to do? Everyone probably chalks it up to placebo, but it's not a placebo! Something is severely wrong! And it's not just us. You've read all the forums, too! And I hear all the jokes about allergies and sensitivities. It's supposed to be so hilarious. If you're not just accepting whatever your doctor says and popping his prescription pills, it's like you're a complete moron, you know?"

With childish sentiment, I continued, "I'm sick of it."

Truthfully, even though I *was* sick of it, I was using my food frustrations to fashion myself into yet another kind of victim. It was a distraction to invite sympathy from Ashley and somehow awkwardly lessen the effects of betrayal. I did the same with chastity. Her acknowledgment of my plight was comforting. Was I trying to force codependency?

The ego is heartless.

FDA-Approved Psychosis

Over the next year, Ashley and I settled on middle ground: foods that did not seem to trigger arthritis but were not on the strict AIP diet. This compromise ebbed and flowed as we guessed our way through a pseudo-elimination regimen and tried to pour into our marriage. At one point, we had just ended a depressing conversation about the profoundly different needs of men and women. We conceded that God is the only answer to a sustainable, healthy marriage. Yet, walking in faith, praying for constant grace, and submitting to His will seemed far too difficult. Admittedly, the alternative was difficult as well. We also wondered why husbands are the most challenging projects for wives and vice versa. As Ashley noticed the time on her phone, she segued.

"What are you going to have for lunch?" Ashley asked.

"I don't know," I responded. "Maybe a tuna salad. You?"

"Nothing sounds good. I'm hungry but can't think of a thing."

"Want me to grab that veggie tofu dish from the Thai place?" I asked.

"Sure. Can you please make sure they skip the sauce?" Ashley reminded me.

"You got it," I said as I left the house. I jumped in the car and drowned myself in worship music, not wanting to think about any more of my past secrets or excuses. As I waited for Ashley's food, I was prompted to text her with a simple note. It read: *Thank you for always working on us. You could've given up a long time ago, but you keep fighting. I love you.*

A nice moment. Then, as quickly as it appeared, it was gone.

Then came an argument. Then feelings of inadequacy. Then a bad meal, followed by wisdom, forgiveness, and disturbing, accusatory thoughts. Then came a good meal. Sometimes in predictable order, other times shuffled. Optimism and joy, then pessimism and anguish.

Repent. Rebuke. Recite. Rehearse. Regret. Rejoice. Recommit. Regress.

Too much fat, too little bone broth, too little fiber, not enough green tea, too many Brussels sprouts, too few spices, not enough organ meats. Try FODMAP. Research Keto. Don't forget Paleo! Pivot left—no, right! No, left again. Too far! Turn back, retrace your steps. Nausea. Confession. Should've had a supplement this morning. Should've exercised more. Should keep a food diary. Should've remembered the multi-vitamin. Should've

8. Death To Self: Autoimmunity

avoided processed snacks. Oops, bloating. Diarrhea. Irritability. More confession. Nausea. Go to jail. Go directly to jail. Do not pass Go. Do not collect $200.

In addition, there were dozens of instances where all was apparently well with my stomach, then I mistakenly or foolishly ate something inflammatory, and all hell broke loose. My thoughts were suddenly foggy, my joints achy, and my mood severely compromised. I described my symptoms as "hollow brain and stomach." It was an odd sensation where I felt my mind floated away and took my gut with it. Usually, these instances occurred when Ashley and I were on an upswing.

"Thanks for helping me around the house today, sweetheart," Ashley said while out to dinner for the first time in months.

"No problem," I responded with a smile. I proceeded to order eggs (not AIP), hash browns (not AIP), and sausage links (from a corner diner—clearly not AIP). I think I polished it off with a gluten-free cookie from the grocery store down the road. Pseudo-elimination had become, "If it looks good and sounds somewhat healthy, it's okay." Rebellion was winning again.

Within an hour, I was short-tempered and couldn't explain why. Once short-tempered, a poor view of Ashley arose. Then anger. Then selfishness. She was left puzzled, wondering where Dr. Jekyll had gone.

So what did I do in response? I blamed food. Yes, food. My new scapegoat.

Trying to remain optimistic while guessing which foods triggered an inflammatory response rivaled the sickening cycle of scrupulous confession.

How is this fair? I cried. Then a whisper: *Keep going.*

Humiliated, I returned to a strict AIP diet. Once again, my *do not* list was crushing: caffeine, alcohol, dairy, gluten, sugar, social media, masturbation, and television—with no carefree money to spend. Alone with my thoughts, I was an ascetic with my tail still fused between my legs. Because of my exposure to so many pleasures in life, the loss of them—however staggered and asymmetric—was nearly intolerable.

Imprisoned again.

Yet, in my old life, even when I occupied the Garden of Earthly Delights, I knew something was missing, so I concluded, *All this denial must be good, right? Maybe I'm finally learning to rely on God, not things.* King Solomon, having acquired any and everything desirable to man, remained unsatisfied, acknowledging in Ecclesiastes 12, verses 13-14: "The end of the matter; all has been heard. Fear God, and keep his commandments; for this is the whole duty of man. For God will bring every deed into judgment, with every secret thing, whether good or evil."

In the background, I whispered, *I need a job; I need my marriage restored; I need to know your will; please release me, Lord.*

9. EPIPHANY: SUFFICIENT GRACE

But he said to me, "My grace is sufficient for you, for my power is made perfect in weakness." I will all the more gladly boast of my weaknesses, that the power of Christ may rest upon me.

—2 Corinthians 12:9

During some random hour, day, and month, Ashley and I were again in the midst of another deep, dark valley. We had been distanced for an extended period of time, urgently trying to bridge our contrasting needs without expressing irritability or abrasiveness. Somehow, the grace of restraint was alive and well in both of us.

"Don't you sense when something's off?" Ashley asked despondently.

Without answering her question, I responded, "Why are you just bringing this up now?"

She hesitated. "I didn't say anything earlier because I was scared of how you'd react. Honestly, it's a lose-lose situation. I feel like either I say something and sacrifice our relationship, or I don't say anything and sacrifice myself. And not the healthy kind of sacrifice."

I replied, "Well, when my body goes down a certain track, it's difficult to derail it. It makes it hard to sense the tension between my needs and your needs. I do care, though. I really do."

"I get that, but being intimate can be terrifying for me. If I don't feel loved, it makes me feel used. But then when we aren't intimate, I feel more pressure and weight every day, anticipating the next time, which gives me crazy anxiety. Then my need to feel loved is even stronger," Ashley replied. "I hate this."

I quickly responded, "Damn. I'm sorry. This is crazy. If we don't have sex, I start to struggle with urges and rejection. When I'm struggling with those, I feel like I can't show you heartfelt love. The physical part is too strong—and it seems impossible to be vulnerable, as you say, when I feel unwanted. I never felt like you actually desired me."

"I understand what you're saying, but just so you know, our entire marriage—our *entire* marriage—I desired you, but I never really felt loved, just tolerated. I felt like you didn't even like me—like I was a nuisance—so I was terrified to be that vulnerable. How could I give myself to someone who didn't seem to love me? I felt rejected just like you. I never wanted to hurt you." Ashley depressingly said. "I don't know how to solve this."

"Neither do I," I agreed.

But that wasn't true. I knew what I was called to, I just didn't know how to do it. I sat back, realizing I was still pursuing Ashley with a victim's sentiment, internally screaming, *I deserve this!* I certainly didn't think, *I need to ensure she feels adored.*

I desperately needed God's help.

Law & Grace

We always struggled with intimacy. We communicated ad nauseam our entire marriage, each clawing for our missing love-equation integers. Complacency always succeeded active change. Attempts at sweet Post-It notes on the mirror always preceded opportune victimhood. Birthday and anniversary cards were mixed with heartfelt and obligatory sayings, followed by little or no touching. Yearning, then caving. Crying, then settling. My efforts in marriage were always short-lived, stifled by greediness—just like my spiritual life was stifled by rebellion. Every effort excluded my heart.

But now, without my favorite former vices, what is there? My thoughts cannot descend. I must claim my baggage, load it into a rental car, leave the airport, and drive directly to the Lord. As I perform the most difficult act—handing suitcases of lingering sin to Him—He gives me: love, joy, peace, patience, kindness, goodness, faithfulness, gentleness, and self-control.

■ ■ ■

Nearly nine months post-confession, I broke new ground. I was being empathetic without prompting. It remained far from second nature, but it was easier. I knew her pain was real and not a game meant to ruin me; by now, I knew her character. We were working toward something beyond comprehension. And although far from tangible, and mostly hazy, it was known. It was one of the only reasons I was persevering, and maybe it was the same for Ashley.

But my unavoidable convictions continued. My only option: trust God, then speak.

"I could tell she was wearing something tempting, so I glanced at her face, peripherally capturing her top half. I wanted to know if the face matched the body," I said. "It's not like I was doing it on purpose. It's a subconscious habit. It feels involuntary."

Like so many confessions, it was seemingly small, yet so raw. A very strange look into my fallen-man impulses. I was a mechanical watch with all gears exposed, set in a display window for Ashley's viewing—and my own. Previously, only the watchmaker Himself knew such intricacies.

Incredibly, however, Ashley was now rebounding quickly. It was *my* response to her momentary sadness or insecurity that dug a new trench between us. When I saw a smile leave her face, I fell in anger. I expected her to listen to my battles without emotion. It was much easier to embrace irritability, which paired well with my stunted memory. I never seemed to recognize that we had been there before. This type of exchange had already happened many times, and I knew the right path to take—to step into her pain and love her in the middle of it—but I didn't take it.

Often, in a state of denial, I'd swap our positions, turning Ashley's grief into mine, insisting my pain was more justified. I often thought, *This is stupid. I'm the rejected one, not her. I'm not doing what I used to do. I've changed!*

Instead of comforting her, I essentially stole her agony, wrapped myself in it, then expected her to sympathize with me—which left her speechless.

Conveniently, I'd replay our conversations and only see a blur. I rarely knew why I responded the way I did.

As a result, intimacy remained non-linear. Even when I tried my best to prioritize Ashley's needs, I'm not sure we were getting it right. I still found a way to sidestep deep emotions and pick up superficiality. It seemed the stars and the planets needed to align in order for us to meet each other's needs. In these rare, precious moments, Biblical love and respect were natural by-products. Each time, I was convinced we had arrived.

9. Epiphany: Sufficient Grace

"Thank you for caring," Ashley said, "even though it seems complicated. I know it's difficult, but thank you."

"Thanks for saying that. It's getting easier," I said.

"What is? Communicating?" she asked.

"Yeah. I used to get lost in my head, overthinking your needs. Now I get it. I just need to remember to not overthink." *Although that sounds like more thinking*, I thought.

Regardless, as soon as the clarity appeared, it was gone. The consequences of betrayal were as unpredictable as a bouncing football.

Conjugal Wrongs

Whether any given occasion of intimacy went as planned or not, its effects carried to the following day.

When things fell into place, Ashley and I embraced in the morning, eager to talk about the upcoming day. However, as soon as a disagreement arose, I sadly refused to parlay our recent improvements. Instead, I failed to acknowledge my part of any given problem. I didn't want to apologize for anything. Therefore, within hours, we were awkwardly distanced, each fighting to ensure our resulting frustrations did not carry further. If they did, a week or two could easily go by before we attempted to be intimate again. In between, of course, there were triggers, confessions, torment, and temptations.

When things fell apart, the next morning was miserable. Ashley sat in bed while I pitied myself as far away from her as possible. I didn't want to talk about it. I didn't want to force some type of fake affection. I just wanted to get on with the day, so I'd eventually roll out of bed, say a half-hearted "Good morning," and get in the shower. I'd often forget (or refuse) to kiss her. This was how I pouted. Within the first hour of the day, I'd know I wasn't willing to attempt anything that night—it would take too much thought and sacrifice. I knew if I tried anything without the appropriate mindset, our progress would suffer. But that wasn't enough to stop my streak of disordered reactions. If I felt rejected on the very night I wasn't willing to try anything anyway, I sulked. Textbook manipulation.

There were many nights where something seemed off, yet we fought to embrace. It was a dual (or duel) sacrifice where Ashley didn't feel great physically, mentally, or emotionally, yet she was willing to try. I only felt urges, yet I prepared to temper them, reminding myself of what she had shared in the past. As we attempted to be intimate one particular night, she paused with trepidation, knowing something was off.

I wasn't expressing love.

I immediately consulted my brain and heard recurring questions: *Are you kidding me?! How am I screwing this up? Is this seriously happening again?*

My emotions skyrocketed as I severed our embrace. I stared at the ceiling while Ashley stared at me, forming typical perpendicular lines of vision. One of us was willing to work through an issue while the other sank in self-pity.

"You're rejecting me," I said.

Ashley replied, "Are you seriously getting mad at me? I just need reassurance. I'm not rejecting you."

"I think we should stop," I responded with full juvenility. "I'm too mad. This isn't going well."

"Honey, I wasn't trying to stop anything. I'm willing to try again if you're able to reset," she replied.

"I don't think I can," I said, as I shook my head.

Ashley jumped back in. "Do you seriously expect me to never say anything? I need to be able to share how things are affecting me without you completely shutting down."

"This affects me, too! Do you realize how many times I

9. Epiphany: Sufficient Grace

haven't gotten things 'just right' for you? Do you have any idea how many times you've made me feel like a failure?" I retorted.

She thought for a second, then replied, "Do you have any idea how many times I haven't gotten things 'just right' for you?! I constantly feel like I'm letting you down! Do you realize how many times *you've* made me feel like a failure? I feel like I'll never be good enough—like I'll never meet your expectations. On top of that, when love is absent, I feel violated and used. I've said it before—it's like I'm not viewed as a person, just a body. If you were actually in a place of love, my insecurity wouldn't make you feel rejected! In fact, if you were truly loving me, don't you think I'd feel it and therefore feel secure and be more in sync with you?"

"This is ridiculous. It's so complicated," I insisted.

She shot back, "It really isn't. I admit I've had moments of intense insecurity, and I realize they're heightened because of this insane process, but my need for love has *always* been like this. It's how I function. It's how women function. I need to feel love from you. If you're annoyed with me, if you resent me, if you're only lusting, I know it. I can feel it. It overrides all other emotions. How can you expect me to feel safe with you when you aren't being loving?"

"How can you expect me to show love when it doesn't feel like you even want to be here with me?" I asked, hoping for an abrupt end to our ping-pong match. "Why can't you just know I love you? Why do you need constant reassurance?"

"I do want to be here. And of course I need reassurance! Do you have any idea how difficult this is for me? Constant flashbacks and images trying to get at me. I swear, I've been fighting through hell this whole time, just like you. If I wanted to give up, I would have. I know your needs–very well at this point. I'm trying to meet them, but I can't pretend everything is fine when it isn't. I need to feel love. And not just now—throughout the day."

"I'm showing you love the way I know how. I've listened to your needs and I'm doing my best to show I care. I'm not perfect!"

"I'm not expecting perfection. You know that. Forgive me if this sounds harsh—I am not trying to sound harsh or disrespectful in any way—but I need you to lead. Remember your comments about the man leading his wife? It applies here. I can't move first without it further damaging our relationship. It's impossible."

As I turned away with a visible swallow of pride, I muttered, "Okay. Let me think about that." I often took five to ten minutes to process a given issue, during which time Ashley's blood pressure spiked. She had no idea what I was thinking, and it scared her. Finally, a whisper from the Holy Spirit said, *She's right. I needed to lead.* Such a confirmation was familiar, but this time it struck marrow.

"You're right," I admitted. "I'll pray and figure out how to move forward." With a heavy sigh, I added, "This is so tough."

Then—as expected—I retreated to my thoughts:

She wants me to lead? I thought I was leading. I thought I was viewing her correctly. I don't want to say I'm wrong. I've admitted I was wrong hundreds—thousands—of times. How can I be so wrong? It must be because I'm humble and she's proud. Is there no quota on this stuff? I'm being called to extreme discipline and obedience at the absolute worst time. Remove all my vices and at the same time be the most mature and affectionate I've ever been?

It felt like twenty minutes had passed by the time I regrouped and turned to Ashley with a smile. We were both trying.

"Thank you, sweetheart," she said. "I know we'll get through this."

As I fell asleep, a final thought hovered: *What is love? Seriously.*

10. DEATH TO SELF: INSANITY

When I am afraid, I put my trust in thee.

—Psalm 56:3

In the early fall of 2017, only four weeks after my first confession to Ashley and the nightmarish lunch interview, several opportunities were in queue. The most promising had just concluded I was a top-four, not a top-two candidate. This was after a series of six interviews with everyone from the tasting room manager to the CEO. However, because they were a publicly-traded company, it didn't surprise me. The same thing happened a decade earlier when I tried to enter the beer industry: six interviews with a single employer, then a demoralizing dismissal.

Ashley was torn. On one hand, she was used to me being home. Although our conversations were often gut-wrenching, we were subtly bonding. She was learning about the real me, and was scared to lose any sliver of that. Our growth would vanish if she lost me for forty to fifty hours a week. In addition—exhausted from the emotional chaos—she valued my help with the kids. On the other hand, she knew the limits of our finances and my intense desire to provide for the family.

Several opportunities fell apart after first interviews, due to disinterest from either of us. Most opportunities died at the last minute, due to strange reasons. One after another. Three of the oddest ones involved employers effectively committing to me, then replying on the week I was expecting a contract:

- "Eddie, I'm sorry, but we've changed the location of the job."
- "It was a tough decision, but we've decided to hire someone from within."
- "My plan was to have this work, but we are now abandoning the position."

In every instance, salary and benefits had been reviewed, the employers were visibly excited, and I had received strong verbal intent. In the past, this would have resulted in two offers, not zero.

Still, LinkedIn inquiries persisted, and I responded to every request. Strangely, I refused to reach out to others; I wanted them to want me. For those who reached out to me, I wanted them to know how awesome I was and how the salary I desired was not only acceptable, it was talent at a discount! I assumed the driver's seat because we had savings in the bank.

It was foreign to be so desperate for a respite, yet uncompromising in my convictions. In the moment, it made little sense, but landing the wrong job seemed more burdensome than at-home torment. At last I'd be able to avoid a thoughtless rebound job. Plus, statistically, there was enough new interest to give me assurance something ideal would strike soon.

In the past, each rejection would've driven me to a bar for a couple of Moscow Mules or home for a half-bottle of wine. But,

10. Death To Self: Insanity

instead of drenching in sadness, I was now swaddling in vanity. I'm sure Ashley took notice. I was a broken man on our couch and an overconfident man leaving for interviews.

{More scrupulous confession}

My fig leaves were apparently screaming at some people.

At coffee, my buddy Jeremy bluntly said, "I've got to be honest. I heard from two different people in the industry that you're coming across as a 'jack of all trades, master of none.' And you seem to have a chip on your shoulder."

"Dang it," I sighed. "That's disappointing to hear."

"Can I give you some advice?" Jeremy asked.

"Sure. Go ahead."

"You're coming across as if you're gunning for CEO. If people think you have *all* the answers, it will seem too good to be true. You need to be humble. I hope you understand I feel comfortable telling you this because you're a friend."

"Yes, I do. I appreciate it. I'm just confused because I was so close to landing three different jobs. If I was such a poor match, I wouldn't have made it to the final stage of interviews."

Jeremy replied, "Wait—didn't you say those discussions were over a month ago? Maybe you're getting desperate and overemphasizing your abilities."

On the way home, Jeremy's words echoed. His perspective was dead on. I was insecure and egotistical—an amateur magician, looking for audience approval for every little skill exhibited. With real confidence and humility, I would've zeroed in on a few strengths and not needed to patch every single hole. Predictably, I was doing what I had done my entire career.

The humiliation of daily confession was not translating outside our house. Instead, it forced remaining impurities to the surface, which chaotically grasped at one last hurrah.

At home, I approached Ashley, saying, "Jeremy told me I'm being perceived as a conceited, do-it-all, know-it-all."

"I'm sorry," Ashley said. "But do you think they're accurate?"

"At first, I thought it was a stupid perspective, but now I realize their perceptions are all that matter. They're holding the cards, not me. But, yeah, I think they're right."

■ ■ ■

Now five months into interviews—after many more disappointments—I felt called to consult. I drafted my business statement and shared it with some industry friends. Very soon, I was in no man's land. I had been so sure that God was telling me to consult, when in reality, it was likely my selfish desire to own a business and carry an attitude of *I'll show them!* I was too proud to admit I didn't know how to launch a consulting business. The potential for failure was so high, I abandoned my poorly devised plan after three weeks.

I was left in crisis. No work, mixed with the weight of ongoing radical confession, diet, and pursuit of chastity, reduced me to something I'll never be able to explain.

At this time, my parents and mother-in-law helped us financially, creating a different kind of nakedness. I was grateful for the support, yet embarrassed, baffled, and livid heading into 2018. Ashley was grateful and—strangely—very calm. She was beginning to trust God's will in a new, powerful way.

Inconceivable!

In January, I felt the presence of God urging me to stop. To finally stop resisting Him—with work, money, and my future. I whiningly responded, *Do you know how much I've obeyed? Just look at what I've said to Ashley. Look at what I've purged. Look at the measures I've taken. Now I'm supposed to surrender more? How?*

10. Death To Self: Insanity

I had grown comfortable as Moses and Aaron, crediting my efforts, echoing, "Must *I* bring you water from this rock?"

My wine career was over. As difficult as it was to accept, that much I knew. My will of a high salary and a fancy job title was to submit to His will of _____. It was fitting to hear this after seeing how many opportunities had disappeared. I then wrestled new thoughts: *Am I creating this voice? Am I so stubborn I had to create excuses by using God? Am I too embarrassed to pursue work after many rejections? Why is God saying I should leave wine? Should I start applying everywhere? Is God saying I shouldn't work, and direction will come later? Is God going to leave me where I am?*

Then the loudest silence. For weeks.

Finally, while anxiously praying, a whisper: *Healthcare admin.*

I fought the impression immediately. *What does that even mean? Is it a job that will fall in my lap or do I need to start making calls? Doesn't God know I have a background in marketing and strategy? Doesn't He know how difficult it would be to jump industries and job roles? What does an admin do anyway? I don't remember.*

I was then convicted to close my LinkedIn account—the very engine feeding me ninety percent of my work opportunities. Most headhunters, former colleagues, and prospective employers could no longer contact me. When friends asked about my job situation, I'd smile, saying, "I believe I'm called to healthcare." I left out the admin part because I apparently knew better than God. I at least wanted to salvage my marketing background.

Through sharing these convictions, friends of friends connected me with three of the top healthcare companies in the state. During interviews, refusing to leave God out of the story, I acknowledged my faith journey and told them all I felt called to their industry. One understood, one paused on the other end of the line, and one kindly cut the interview short. Not one interview led to a follow-up. Nausea permeated. *Familiar.*

However, there was Ashley, reminding me to keep walking regardless of perceived rejection or disaster.

■ ■ ■

For an early Valentine's Day meal, Ashley and I went to our favorite restaurant, Mission Heirloom—the only one we had ever found specifically designed to address an array of diet protocols.

We ordered our food and sat down near the entrance. Ashley reached into her purse and pulled out her gift to me: a small wooden box with a booklet inside. Page after page contained Bible verses about children, marriage, and God's love. The second-to-last page read, "...I tell you the truth, if you had faith even as small as a mustard seed...nothing would be impossible" (Matthew 17:20). The final page had an actual mustard seed inside a heart with the statement above: Due 10-22-18.

Grinning, eyes welling with tears, I asked, "Really?"

The thought of Baby #3 was amazing, yet horrifying. I was to be financially responsible for a family of five, I hadn't had a job in seven months, and I had recently deleted LinkedIn. *That's nice*, I thought. *How will I support the family now?*

Less than two weeks later, several wine jobs surfaced. I received an email from a recruiter, a call from a friend, and a text from an old employer—all excited to discuss slam-dunk opportunities. Even those that were not outright offers were so promising, so obvious, that I'd have either been scary stupid or scary faithful to pass them up. Hesitantly, but with the best obedience I could summon, I declined these opportunities—one after another, with the best being a job and title I had always thought I desired.

I remember asking Ashley, "I heard clearly, right? Did I *say* I heard God clearly?"

At the same time, I envisioned friends and family asking

10. Death To Self: Insanity 149

themselves, "If he's having trouble getting work, is he too good for Burger King? AMPM is hiring. So is Whole Foods, the corner pet clinic, the dry cleaners. So is EVERYWHERE else. Unemployment is at a forty-eight-year low! What is wrong with him?"

Just imagine if they knew the truth, I told myself. *How can I rest knowing we accepted money from family? Why should our faith journey impact others' finances? As soon as we can, we are paying them back. This is ridiculous.* I then began to question every purchase we had made since I lost my job.

Around this time, an online story—"Rescue"—jumped off my screen:

A very religious man was once caught in rising floodwaters. He climbed onto the roof of his house and trusted God to rescue him. A neighbor came by in a canoe and said, "The waters will soon be above your house. Hop in, and we'll paddle to safety."

"No thanks," replied the religious man. "I've prayed to God, and I'm sure he will save me."

A short time later, the police came by in a boat. "The waters will soon be above your house. Hop in, and we'll take you to safety."

"No thanks," replied the religious man. "I've prayed to God, and I'm sure he will save me."

A little time later, a rescue services helicopter hovered overhead, let down a rope ladder, and said, "The waters will soon be above your house. Climb the ladder, and we'll fly you to safety."

"No thanks," replied the religious man. "I've prayed to God, and I'm sure he will save me."

All this time the floodwaters continued to rise until soon they reached above the roof, and the religious man drowned. When he arrived at heaven, he demanded an audience with God. Ushered into God's throne room, he said, "Lord, why am I here in heaven? I prayed for you to save me, I trusted you to save me from that flood."

"Yes, you did, my child," replied the Lord. "And I sent you a canoe, a boat, and a helicopter. But you never got in."

■ ■ ■

Was each job opportunity a canoe? A boat? A helicopter? Should I be working as a GM or VP right now? Who is dumb enough to pass up these opportunities? This is exactly what I wanted.

These thoughts caused regret, strangely followed by solace. I reminded myself I had grown to KNOW when I was resisting God's will—and this fact exceeded everything, no matter how ignorant it appeared. Nevertheless, this would've been a good time for wise counsel. At the time, however, it completely escaped me. I only saw a tunnel and God's hand reaching for me.

Every few weeks, my faith plummeted and my desperation soared. Yet—every time—I either heard "rest" or nothing at all. I continually asked: *How long can this possibly continue?* I was often thinking about others and their views of me. Each passing month was another lead vest—more people judging me, wondering why I was not working two to three jobs if unable to match previous work, thinking I was entitled, wondering how Ashley and I maintained a strict diet with supplements, wondering why I seemed to lack a sense of urgency. The anguish and confusion melded well with everything else.

But just as quickly as intense negativity flooded my head, it dissipated; I knew there was no other way. Even if Ashley and I had missed some of God's cues along the way, we were still on the right path. I was convinced of this many times.

To remain in (or return to) sanity, I juxtaposed "Rescue" with the story of Lazarus. Upon hearing of Lazarus' sickness, Jesus "stayed where he was two more days" even though He knew what Mary and Martha wanted. Likewise, I knew what the collective Mary and Martha thought was best for me—heck, most

10. Death To Self: Insanity

everyone would've shouted, "Take any job, you clown!" And while I couldn't fathom the reasoning behind turning down jobs, chasing God's will was all that mattered.

{More scrupulous confession}

Then more colleagues called, asking if I was still available for work, and I was compelled to tell them I was being called out of wine. Because I knew money was either on the table or close by, these conversations reeked of nonsense. I pictured people reprimanding me, stating Bible verses: "If a man doesn't work, he shall not eat" and "But those who won't care for their relatives, especially those in their own household, have denied the true faith."

These thoughts broke me. I questioned my stability, only to conclude, *If I'm insane, would I even be able to question my sanity? Would I even know that I had gone to the other side? How far can all of this go?*

At my lowest, Ashley confidently approached me, breaking my daydream spiral. "Honey, you are working! You are providing. You're busting your butt, buying groceries, making meals, doing laundry and dishes, playing with the kids, and fighting for our marriage. Cut yourself some slack!"

Her words meant a lot, especially at a time when she and I were in one of our many communication valleys. Still, it was numbing to realize the easier choice—a well-paying job that seemed to serve disobedience—appeared more Scripturally sound.

Months passed, and now even the healthcare directive was cloudy. Wine was not an option—that much remained clear. Therefore, I was left with a recurring, frustrating question: *WHAT am I supposed to do?!* I wanted to pray and recite Scripture in these moments, but more often than not, I was paralyzed.

One thing kept me focused hour to hour, day to day, week to week: whispers.

Rest. Stay where you are. This is good.

Surreal Estate

"I'm not accepting any more money from my family or yours. That's it!" I told Ashley. "I know how much they care, but I can't ask or accept from them again. We need to figure this out. *Why am I being told not to work?*"

We had eighty-six dollars in the bank, then sixty-one dollars, then one hundred forty dollars. A few times, we went into the red while scrambling to sell something. There was the time Ashley's rheumatologist covered the cost of her appointment as a gift; the time Ashley's friend gave us one hundred dollars because she felt God told her to; the time we were given some kids' clothes for free; and so on.

Turning our garage from graveyard to goldmine, we sold a bed, a couch, a grill, chairs, a crib mattress, a play kitchen, patio furniture, strollers, and a dozen other items. We decided whether Craigslist or a virtual yard sale Facebook group would be the better option, then created a listing and waited. We also liquidated our short-lived wine brand, withdrew funds from our 401(k), and sold both our cars so we could get a used Pathfinder.

It was then time to sell our only remaining asset: our house. It didn't matter if Napa was set to become the greatest housing market in the world; we simply needed cash. We used most of our remaining money to hire subcontractors to fix our bathtub, shower, fence, and plumbing—areas we knew would be red flags during a showing.

We knew of these potential issues because we had listed our house years earlier in 2015, but—due to taking Dave Ramsey's Financial Peace University classes—realized the hastiness of our

10. Death To Self: Insanity

decision. Within two weeks, we took our house off the market. We wanted to sell our 1,250 sq. ft. home in order to purchase a 1,600 sq. ft. home a few miles away. We would've considerably increased our debt, interest payments, and stress—all for an extra room.

But this time the motive was quite different. On Easter Sunday, April 1, 2018, our house hit the market again.

We accommodated every viewing request, which included three open houses and an additional fifteen to twenty groups. The house was left spotless, while the garage was littered with cleaning supplies, trash cans, and toys.

During this time, despite underlying issues, Ashley and I were bonding in a new way. We spiritually held hands as we walked into what we understood to be God's will. Through mutual faith, He was sewing our torn fabric.

On April 15, an offer was made, then—due to earthquake concerns—retracted a few hours later.

{More scrupulous confession}

A few days later, new groups expressed interest. The most promising prospects wanted to visit a second time on April 22, at a specific time in the afternoon, so it could be determined whether backyard sunlight was ideal for planting a garden. That morning, however, I found both our bathtub and shower basin filled to the brim with sewage, and immediately called off the showing. Still, I refused to call a plumber, concerned about the cost.

I returned to the bathrooms around 4 p.m. to find both areas emptied! With a strange smirk, I rushed to disinfect the layered, clinging remains. I knew there was a chance the prospective buyers would stop by and make an offer, so I called our agent to inform him we were open to show the house if they were still available.

A half hour later, we drove the kids to a nearby park while

the interested party took a final look. Apparently, they were very enthusiastic; nevertheless, we held our breaths.

As my stubbornness wore off, I knew our plumbing issue would persist and feared the next flush would create a bigger problem, so I called Roto-Rooter that night and paid the emergency fee of $295.

On April 24, a new offer came in: listing price *plus* forty-five-day escrow *plus* two weeks of free rent back.

Thank you, Lord.

The free rent back was completely unexpected, but greatly appreciated because of our dwindling money. However, the extended escrow was going to make the final two weeks nearly impossible to financially navigate. But, instead of voicing our opinion, we stayed silent, not wanting to rock the boat. Without recourse, we could only sit and wait. We prayed for every inspection to be completed without cause for concern and for contingencies to be lifted quickly.

Absurdly, even if everything went as planned, we didn't know our next destination.

■ ■ ■

On May 17, Ashley and I were back at Mission Heirloom, returning from a rheumatologist appointment in San Francisco. Given our financial situation, we should've skipped the restaurant, but as I well knew, when my stomach was leading the charge, money was no object.

"Oh my gosh!" we heard, as Laura approached us. "What are you guys doing here?!"

"You're the one who told us about this place! What are *you* doing here? Don't you live, like, two hours away?" Ashley responded while hugging Laura.

10. Death To Self: Insanity

"Yeah. I stop here any time I'm heading to San Francisco. Can you believe they're closing today?"

"Yeah, we just heard. This was our spot," Ashley said sadly.

I added, "This is where Ashley told me she was pregnant a few months ago."

Smiling, we sat down to an early dinner, anxious to finally catch-up in person. We had been virtually meeting for well over a year. Within minutes, I began sharing portions of our journey, mostly related to my job situation.

Still reluctant to be too specific, I said, "I feel called to healthcare, in some capacity."

Laura's eyes lit up. "No kidding! Hmm...I'm not sure if you remember, but in addition to my own practice, I work for a separate company. They might need someone like you. Remind me of your experience."

Within a few weeks, I was interviewed by Laura's employer's marketing department. Lasting over an hour, I thought the discussion was promising. However, a follow-up never happened. I decided to leave it alone, knowing it didn't fit the admin bill anyway.

■ ■ ■

Once all contingencies were lifted, we prematurely exhaled. Only a week from closing, we were advised of a potential delay: a third party needed to sign, and there was nothing we could do to speed the process. Because we were down to a few hundred dollars, we negotiated to receive a small amount of the proceeds in advance while the issue was sorted.

On June 15, our fifty-two-day escrow closed.

Shortly thereafter, we learned the buyers had considered bailing. During the contingency phase, we paid for an external bypass line to be installed in our plumbing system. Because our house was more than fifty years old, this requirement was long overdue. During the installation, a comprehensive evaluation was conducted, and the report disclosed the rest of our plumbing was in excellent shape. However, if we had not had the sewage issue in April, we would not have had the pipes cleaned, and if the pipes had not been cleaned, the buyers would've backed out. They had previously been burned by a severe plumbing issue, so anything less than pristine would've ended the contract.

Sewage *can* be a blessing.

On the afternoon of the fifteenth, sale proceeds hit our bank account. But our relief was short-lived, as reality slapped us again. We needed a house by June 29.

Onward and hopeful, we searched. Because I didn't have a job, we were forced to rent and provide proof of our savings. No landlord would accept us otherwise.

We felt led to Vacaville, forty minutes east of Napa. Vacaville was where we first attended church together and was home to many of our closest friends. It was a reasonable next step: lower cost of living, still close to Ashley's family, and potentially right down the street from our church.

A day later, on the night of the sixteenth, Ashley leaned toward me, saying, "I trust you."

Over the next two days, we viewed the widest possible range of homes. The following Tuesday we found a great spot, made an offer, and were convinced we had it secured. It fell through a few days later. We went back to the drawing board, realizing most of the options listed on Zillow and Craigslist would not be vacant for another six to eight weeks.

{More scrupulous confession}

As we regrouped, I expanded our search by increasing our monthly budget by a few hundred dollars. This time a gem appeared. The rental agent, Ahmed, who lived two hours away and was only in town once a week, happened to be in the area when I called. We drove out to meet him and were amazed by his professionalism, as well as the condition of the house and its proximity to the freeway. He disclosed that the house had been listed for six weeks because the owners were extremely selective with tenants.

After chatting with us for thirty minutes, Ahmed assured us we had a chance. The next day, we submitted an application, and—in our desperation—offered to pay extra up-front. The rest of the proceeds were budgeted for remaining rental costs, other monthly expenses, and a certificate-of-deposit account. Not knowing what the future held, we desired a conservative investment. We knew we were blessed to have such an option.

Still, cynical thoughts circled, as I shook my head: *We are seriously supposed to live off of our house proceeds? That could be used to purchase our next house or secure some of our retirement! I turned down jobs for this?! This is the opposite of everything I've learned about money.*

A day later, we heard from Ahmed:

"Mr. Trask, I'm so sorry. It's not going to work. You can't rent due to an HOA restriction. The owners made a mistake and didn't realize the stipulations. Honestly, I don't understand, but I wanted to call you as soon as possible."

"Dang it," I dismally responded. "Well—thanks for all your help."

"Keep looking. You'll find something. I'm sure of it. Again, I'm sorry."

Inside, Ashley and I were crushed, but we had no time to grieve. With zero prospects, we had one week left to find a house. Panic set in as we frantically called other rental properties in the area.

Remarkably, on the morning of Monday, the twenty-fifth, Ahmed followed up:

"Mr. Trask, you're not going to believe this. We worked out

the HOA issue! If you'd like, you're free to move in today. I'll email the rental contract immediately."

"Seriously?! Yes!" I yelled, as I ran inside to tell Ashley and the kids.

On Wednesday night—in our new living room—I shook my head, laughed, then looked at Ashley and asked, "What are we doing? This is nuts."

Coup De Grâce

In July 2018, having been without a job for a year, I ran into an old friend at church. I shared my story, expecting the same confused look I had seen dozens of times, but instead he said, "I'm in healthcare—*and* I'm an administrator."

"That's incredible," I responded. "Do you remember my experience?"

He continued, "Yes—I sure do. There may be plans to promote me soon. You could possibly become an intern groomed to take my place. Regardless, I think we can find something for you."

This quickly led to a series of interviews, along with enthusiasm and validation about hearing from the Holy Spirit. *This is it! This is finally happening!* In fact, I was so convinced it was God's will, I decided no matter the job, title, or pay, I would take it.

Because they didn't have an immediate opening for administrator-in-training, I was asked if I'd be interested in interim part-time work. The openings were dishwasher, receptionist, and security guard—and like a gambler who plays several blackjack hands at once, I applied for all three.

Less than a week later, I interviewed with two department heads and a human resources director—again, sharing what I felt was appropriate. As expected, as my story progressed, the collective attitude was one of bewilderment. They asked about the possibility of on-call work, assuring it wasn't a deal breaker.

10. Death To Self: Insanity

I responded I could work any shift between 5 a.m. and 6 p.m., placing priority on evenings with the family and anticipating the coming months with a newborn. I was convinced employer inflexibility would've crushed our marital progress, so I tried my best to offer the widest range of hours. But, in that very moment, I envisioned people saying, "Beggars can't be choosers—you should offer to work 24-7! What is wrong with you?"

As I had many times by then, I went home and prayed, ending with, "Father, thy will be done. If this is not supposed to happen, please let it fall to the ground. If it is, please make it obvious."

Within a few days, I was told they had passed on me—for all three jobs. As I sat back in shock, I reflected, *There's no way this is real. This is long past a comedy of errors—it's a dramedy. What have I done? I am ruining our lives. I thought this was it. I really did. I can't even get a job as a dishwasher?*

Again, in one of my darkest moments, Ashley gently said, "I trust you." And this time she added, "God has us."

However, despite Ashley's support, the weight of the latest disappointment led to several months of new misunderstanding, irritation, and isolation. Our marital ups and downs were playing on a loop. Epiphanies were followed by inadequacy and nuisance.

And because excuses for rebellion grow on trees, no matter how seemingly inconsequential, I protested with sugar and caffeine for a week. In the middle of it, I shared yet another nugget of insanity:

"I ran into a liquor store next to the phở restaurant to grab a coke," I explained to Ashley. "As I faced the cashier, I happened to look right and saw a porn magazine display. In plain view. Can you believe it?"

Such a "confession" seemed harmless in advance, but, sadly, its impact was well beyond our expectations. I thought it was a simple comment reminding us of the dangers of relativism and blatant immorality. Like other topics we had discussed, I thought it would lead to a conversation about how we can possibly help other marriages in the future. Instead, Ashley's face sank in heartbreak as she relived the past year.

With tears welling and head slumped, Ashley left the room, whispering, "I'll be back."

And what did I do? I entertained victimhood. I felt like a year's worth of hurts, triggers, and humiliation had suddenly dropped on my lap in a consolidated mess. It felt so unfair. As a result, I focused on *my* feelings.

Why am I asked to share things that hurt so badly? Was I asked, actually? Why would I bring up known triggers? It wasn't a sin, so what good is it? I don't have these issues any longer. Have we not gone through enough of this garbage?

My soda tasted like crap. The carbonation and phosphoric acid hitting my throat did not "hurt so good", as it usually did. I haven't had one since.

Meanwhile, tired of traumatic memories, Ashley called a therapist.

Awake, O Sleeper

Less than a month later, a healthy and happy Zion Trask was born, weighing just over 7 lbs. Ashley and I kissed and held hands as we discussed the past thirteen turbulent months. Considering I never thought I'd be equipped to raise more than two children, I was fairly peaceful the first day.

However, predictably, the day we left the hospital was terrible. About an hour before being discharged, typical anxiety kicked in.

- *How are Arlo and Eviana behaving?*
- *What paperwork did they say we need to sign?*
- *I've already gone to the car three times!*

10. Death To Self: Insanity

- Why does so much junk end up in the trunk?
- As they say, with three kids, you have to switch from man-to-man to zone defense.
- How are we going to do this?

Perhaps the worst of it: I feared impending sleep deprivation would knock us back six months.

On our third night home, having gotten four to six hours of sleep since returning from the hospital, the kids were in bed by 7:30 p.m. An hour later, Ashley finished feeding Zion. And a half hour after that, we were asleep. Roughly forty-five minutes in, the apocalypse began. Zion wailed. Then quieted down. Then wailed again. Then again and again. Then, as she often did, Eviana yelled in her sleep. We hopelessly sat up and shook our heads. I pictured a Navy SEAL instructor yelling, "Get wet and sandy!" at 3:30 a.m. to BUD/S candidates who had just hit a deep NREM sleep. In a stupor, any responsibility seems cruel.

Since Ashley had gotten far less sleep, I volunteered to rock Zion. As I approached Zion's crib, my empathy was already on fumes. Still, I picked him up, gently whispered in his ear, and hugged him. However, he would not calm down. Within minutes, he was inconsolably screaming, with tears streaming down his face. As if he'd answer, I asked, "What's wrong, bud?" Then, as I stood up and positioned him outward, I pleaded, "Chill out, please." Humbly, no matter what I had learned with our first two kids, I couldn't get him to stop, and the lack of sleep was attempting to put me back in my old clothes. Only thirty minutes in, I was mentally cussing, screaming, and kicking. At one point, I forcefully shushed in Zion's ear, and he began to shriek even louder. Then came condemning thoughts: *I'm a horrible father. What is wrong with me?*

Once in that mindset, my head spiraled out of control and thoughts of unforgiveness consumed me. I then welcomed lies about my past, present, and future. *Why is this coming back? I thought all of this had been dealt with.*

Humiliated, I sighed, then fell back in the rocking chair. Yet, instead of praying, I fixated on the mental and emotional energy needed to raise our five-year-old and two-year-old; keep a newborn alive; be a husband to Ashley; and remain disciplined elsewhere. As I rewound our journey, I doubted it entirely, dismissing all the clear signals I had received over the past year.

Somehow, I ended my shift in prayer. When I tapped Ashley on the shoulder to take over, I was too embarrassed to tell her what had just occurred, but knew I would eventually share it.

A day later:

"Nope, his latch is horrible. I think he has ties like Eviana did. He's just gulping air no matter what I do." Ashley said, heartbroken.

"Dang. Well, let's set an appointment. Maybe he won't need a revision, but they can give us some advice," I responded.

"I can almost guarantee he's going to need surgery. I'll call a lactation specialist in the meantime."

Less than a week later, we were at a doctor's office, prepping for Zion's surgery. It took less than thirty seconds and was performed with a cold laser, not a hot one like that used in Eviana's mouth. Less than two minutes after the bittersweet procedure, we exhaled as Zion latched correctly and stopped crying.

{More scrupulous confession}

Then we were reminded: this is only the beginning. To ensure the wounds under Zion's tongue and upper lip healed correctly, we were to perform "exercises" day and night. An alarm would sound at 1 a.m. I'd roll over, slap on nitrile gloves, position my headlamp on the lowest setting, place Zion perpendicular to me, then press my index finger under his lip and swoop side to side. His loud cry enabled me to do the same exercise

10. Death To Self: Insanity

under his tongue. This was repeated every four hours for five weeks straight. In order to cope, I went numb.

When I awoke from the weeks'-long trance that only a newborn could inflict, I felt the weight of unemployment like never before. *I'm now responsible for a family of five*, I repeated.

I need a job; I need my marriage restored; I need to know your will; please release me, Lord.

11. EYES OPEN

I know that thou canst do all things, and that no purpose of thine can be thwarted.

—Job 42:2

In November—distressed with no prospects and little confidence—I received an email from Laura's employer. Without mention of our previous marketing-role discussion, they told me they were considering a part-time virtual assistant and had thought of me as a candidate. I wrote, "I'm very interested!"

On Friday, December 14, at the end of my second FaceTime interview—and after discussing a budgeted hourly rate—the conversation shifted.

"I still don't understand. You have an MBA and over ten years of high-level business experience. *Why* do you want this job?" the business owner asked.

"I feel I'm called to it," I replied.

Clearly surprised, he responded with a chuckle: "Okay then. Sounds good. Well, what hours are you looking for?"

"Since it's part-time, I was hoping for twenty to twenty-five hours a week to start, but anything you deem appropriate is fine," I replied.

"That's perfect. That's exactly what we're looking for," he said. "When can you start?"

I couldn't hide my smile. "Monday."

"Monday it is. We'll send paperwork this weekend."

As I sat back for a moment, it hit me: *I'm a part-time, 1099-employee with no benefits, making a fraction of what I was in the wine industry, working remotely, and I'm happy.* Not only was the job in healthcare administration, but it also allowed me to write this book, continue focusing on family, and transition to reemployment without dramatic change.

Yet, like many ups in this journey, they were followed by aggravating downs. Overcome with self-doubt, I asked, *Is this right? Is this God's will? Will I get fired? How will this provide for the family long-term? God, is this right? Our house proceeds will only last so long.*

It had been seventeen months—seventeen *long* months—without work. Fearful of the adjustment, I recognized I was like "Red" Redding in *Shawshank Redemption*, who said, "These walls are funny. First you hate 'em, then you get used to 'em. Enough time passes, you get so you depend on them. That's institutionalized."

During the job drought, my oldest son had been faithful in asking, always with a grin, "How many days have you been home?" "Now how many days has it been?" "And now?" "How about now?" "Twenty-five days, Daddy?" "Seventy days?" "What? One hundred fifty days?" "Two hundred seventy-five days?" "Four hundred sixty days? Whoa, Dad!"

On Sunday evening, Ashley and I stood in shock as we discussed where to situate my bedroom workstation. The next morning, I sat at my newly purchased, twenty-five-dollar IKEA desk, arranged some fake succulents, positioned my computer, keyboard, and mouse, grabbed a pen and a notepad, and got to work. While recalling the past year and a half, I wanted to cry, but nothing came out. I was disoriented, yet able to see the extraordinary gift in front of us.

During my jobless stint, aside from a few days of travel, Ashley and I had communicated every afternoon during the kids' quiet time for at least an hour and every night for an additional hour. It felt like we had just experienced a decade of marriage counseling. *Maybe that's why God asked me to stay put.*

Less than two weeks later, I positioned a Christmas gift from my father-in-law and stepmother-in-law on the wall just above my desk: Thomas Kinkade's *Walk of Faith*. It features Jesus walking with Peter in an idyllic garden scene. As Peter holds keys in his hand, it is assumed Matthew 16:19 had just been recorded in history. I had no idea what it meant. I just liked its serenity.

If only I knew then what I know now.

Exhausted

Now almost three months postpartum, Ashley and I were again in a deep, dark valley. The normative, doctor-recommended, six-week sex break caused an odd separation, followed by enormous insecurities. As I revisited our past lessons, I remembered the steps necessary to help Ashley feel loved, to view her with the correct lens. Even then, my memory was lacking. I had forgotten her yet again. Chastity had transitioned from gift to curse.

Yet, by grace alone, some optimism survived.

It took sixteen months—sixteen months since the whole ordeal began—before it registered: rather than living with a *shelf life*, what if—by "walking by the Spirit" (Galatians 5:25)—I could escape the selfishness causing many of our fallouts. What if I finally learned to love consistently, without expectation and expiration? Would it finally end our back tracking? I knew loving

Ashley became a chore if even a speck of annoyance entered my head. When insincerely attending her, my core motive remained skewed. This usually meant half-hearted attempts at sacrifice, accomplishing nothing, increasing my frustration, and causing further delays in trust and intimacy.

But this day was different. Ashley and I were in bed chatting while the kids napped. As these thoughts entered my head, I shared them.

"I think I get it," I said, turning to Ashley. "I keep focusing on myself, asking, 'How long has it been since I did this or that? How long must I be good? What have I *not* done?'"

Her joy was restrained. I knew why. I was solving a mystery, so I continued.

"Every question I ask is about my needs and accomplishments. It always revolves around my performance. I have trouble thinking of you because I view you as impossible to please." I looked down in embarrassment. "You're not impossible to please. I am."

Then I asked myself, *What does it take for my love to be sincere? Does it occur when I finally let go of ideals? When I forgive daily? Or when I stop thinking about what I can get out of a situation? I must remain proactive. That's the only way.*

When proactive, I lean on God, fill up on His Word, and pray constantly. When reactive, I lean on flesh, fill up on *my* words, and sulk constantly, which forces me to insist Ashley has miraculously changed her biology, emotions, and habits since we'd last had a discussion or argument.

I neglected time with God—the only One capable to provide the grace, strength, and wisdom needed in these crucial moments. Yet, it was easier to force fake words of appreciation and throw a tantrum when those words fell flat, as they often did. Ashley knew the motives behind my words; she could sniff the slightest falsehood. But I'd force the issue, asking questions like,

11. *Eyes Open*

"Did you not hear me? Do you know how to take a compliment? Why can't you accept my effort?"

At that point, I couldn't pause and humbly ask God to refuel me. The result? Go to jail. Go directly to jail. Do not pass Go. Do not collect $200.

I think I get it now, I said to myself. *I know how to avoid this.* However—like many epiphanies—mistakes and mental harassment were likely to follow. Even if such thoughts were pessimistic and short-sighted, certain patterns were too predictable to ignore.

A Reformed Thesis

From infancy to twenty-three years old, I was Catholic; from twenty-three to twenty-seven, I was a runaway still claiming a belief in God (under my breath); and from twenty-seven to thirty-six, I was a non-denominational Protestant. Through most of it, I was unsettled, ignorant, and proud. Instead of being an obedient, faithful Christian, I was a rebellious child with a malformed thesis.

On Friday, February 8, the flu gripped me. Miserable and quarantined for half the day, I officially "went to bed" around 8:30 p.m. and found myself still awake at 9:30 p.m., 10:30 p.m., 11:30 p.m., 12:30 a.m.—every passing hour reviving traumas of the past year and a half. I just wanted to sleep. Desperate, I counted sheep. Alternating from small to large, cartoon to real, they were helping—kind of. However, at 1:30 a.m., I was wide awake. By then, I was overcome with emotion, praying in intervals of ten to twenty seconds, then losing focus and getting thrown back into wretched torment.

God intervened just after 2 a.m. It wasn't peaceful; like His confrontation at Alston Park, it was a takeover that left me uneasy. He wasn't saying, "confess to your wife"; "rest"; or "stay where you are"—instead, I felt called to continue researching Christian history, specifically Catholicism. The impression was a log rammed into my already stick-laden bicycle spoke.

Still, I fought these overpowering feelings for at least a half hour before I got out of bed to use the restroom. I closed the door and began sobbing, asking God what He wanted from me. My nose and eyes were streaming as I leaned over the toilet. *Father, I will do whatever you need me to do. Please help me. I don't know what's going on. You want me to explore Christianity further? I thought I was doing that. Why is everything so confusing?*

For the better part of three months, I had been studying various Protestant denominations, prompted by some of Ashley's keen doctrinal questions. Sadly, up to that point, most of my life had consisted of going through the motions—first Catholicism, then Protestantism. Consequently, I was clueless about Christian history.

Finally, as I sought to answer Ashley's questions and a new set of my own, I traced many non-denominational churches to Pentecostal and Charismatic movements; then traced Ashley's Seventh Day Adventist upbringing to Baptist movements; then explored Anglican, Methodist, and Presbyterian teachings; then found myself comparing Calvinism, Arminianism, and Molinism. I followed what I thought was a logical progression from one fork—and one splinter—to another.

However, through it all, there was a blockade, making 1517 seem light-years from 1516. It seemed Christ had been crucified in the sixteenth century, so once I arrived at the early Reformer years, I felt I had gone as far as I needed, yet I didn't know what to do next. Only a day before I got sick, I had watched a fascinating John MacArthur sermon series titled: *Saved or Self-Deceived*. Still, as much as I nodded my head in agreement, I wasn't fully convinced of anything. Strangely, no matter how upstream I swam, Catholicism was out of the picture.

Until that February night, when another blindfold fell and dozens of light bulbs flashed, I could not push past this *Reformation Wall*. It was massive and fortified with centuries of stacked offenses, games of telephone, deliberate propaganda and omission, proof-texting, rejection of authority, confused laity, and darkness cleverly and purposefully weaved into pictures, words, and traditions. Church scandal, coupled with one man's decisive renouncement of specific actions, meant the baby, the bath water, and the house itself needed to be thrown out—if not immediately, then over time.

Rebellion won. It always won, even if incrementally.

■ ■ ■

With my pride pulverized and cognitive dissonance exposed, I studied early Christianity to the 1521 Diet of Worms without an angry bias and fear of man. I began to see piecemeal information for what it was—and one by one, each issue I had with the Church was proven misunderstood or misrepresented.

While using a lens five hundred years removed from cataclysmic schism, certain dogmas and practices appeared alien and created apprehension. However, I soon theorized each subsequent Protestant division—combined with popular movie depictions—made vestments, crucifixes, relics, and various doctrines appear all the more sinister and unclear, certainly compared to a modern church service reflecting current culture, style, and concessions. As with Ashley and me, it had become an exponential detachment. Depending on what side one is standing on, and through which lens they're looking, the other seems unrecognizable and increasingly wrong.

Despite it all, I was finally willing to look at Christ and His Body as a whole—no longer obsessed with Judases, Pharisees, and other forms of yeast who love infecting the Church from inside and outside. After that, I studied martyrdom, sainthood, and writings from the early Church Fathers (especially regarding the Holy Eucharist). Then I reviewed my life: what I believed at various times, why I believed it, how I acted as a "Christian," how I used convenience as a crutch, and how a return to Catholicism seemed too challenging, whereas remaining Protestant seemed too easy.

As I learned the hard way, there is a potential problem on both sides of the Tiber River, subject to the Christian pendulum of overcorrection. When I stripped the law of its power, I endorsed subjectivity under the guise of grace; when I stripped grace of its power, I endorsed human effort under the guise of law. In either instance, pride and flesh prevailed.

Additionally, cowardice and hypocrisy exist on both sides. I'm sure I secretly waited to read about any priest or pastor stumbling in sin, only to use the resulting disappointment to catch their tailwind and perpetuate my favorite sins, as if I would not answer to the Judge overseeing it all. It seems any loss of credibility excused my sin, whether I stayed or fled. In either instance, victimhood prevailed.

If I'm led by the Spirit and therefore not under law (Galatians 5:18), yet separated from the Church, such victimhood could necessitate the Church of Eddie. If led by the Spirit, yet separated from the Church, what is objective? My subjective "Holy-Spirit-led" conclusions?

Should I endeavor to create a denomination that perfectly suits me and my findings? Or find someone else's denomination built on their spiritual promptings or doctoral research? Or seek a singular Church, in all her brilliance and crises, appointed by Christ to prevent and contain such potential wildfire autonomy and fragmentation?

Would I then deem such a Church a shepherd or a dictator? Like in a parent-teen relationship, would the Church become a dictator the moment I disagreed with her house rules? Would I

11. Eyes Open

then seek to discredit the rest of her teachings? Would I expect such an institution to only house saints? "All have sinned and fall short of the glory of God" (*except Catholics?*). What if some of the Church's clergy and laity were horribly sinful or superstitious, dismissing many of Christ's teachings? Did their free will cease when they became members of His Church? Does an outlier or standard deviation equal an entire data set or the graph itself? Is the sum of select parts greater than its whole?

When its members acted out and behaved contrary to their callings, would I seek to disparage the Church? Then, for good measure, render it the *Whore of Babylon* based on a "clear" understanding of the Book of Revelation?

If the Bride of Christ has torn ligaments, broken limbs, and punctured lungs, does the Body need to heal, or should it be tossed into a furnace? Likewise, with such a standard, as any subsequent body of believers matures, it too must be discarded as soon as it is injured.

Excuses for rebellion grow on trees.

■ ■ ■

What if the Church experienced a separation? How would I act then? Is any fracture a license to rule myself? Would I abandon ship when judged by others? Or when duplicity surfaced? If that was the case, where would I go? Why would I dare attend any church? While at it, why would I definitively declare anything? At such a point, I could only trust myself, all while using the "Holy Spirit" as my ego's yes-man. My own private, sliding-scale authority.

Additionally, while essentially acting as a pseudo-god, I'm sure mysteries would frustrate me. I bet I'd think, *I must have an explanation for everything on earth. In the meantime, I'll continue calling out falsehoods while remaining free of error.*

But since this was an impossibility, I was left with faith and trust.

Much like Jesus Christ of Nazareth—the One with the often bold, hated, hard-to-accept claims—His Church would be secure in her sacraments and other mysteries. This—added to an unbroken, 2,000-year-long chain of apostolic succession and a pedigree of heresy condemnation—left me leaning toward Catholicism, despite its members' historical and continued failures.

Still, I mock debated in my head, a last-ditch effort to somehow prove Protestantism was right (certainly right enough not to leave it), but I soon recognized I was only left with red-herring fallacies—those which focused on sinful clergy and laity and did nothing to address *actual* Catholic doctrinal and theological teaching; the saints and their heroic virtues; or the futility of self-governance and rampant personal revelations under the guise of *Bible Alone*.

I then considered other questions: did the Twelve Apostles and early Church Fathers foretell or live out Lutheranism? Anabaptism? Calvinism? Did they practice rituals and traditions that couldn't be comprehended until the sixteenth century? Where would you find a second, seventh, or eleventh-century Lutheran teaching? Did Catholic indulgence abuse miraculously unearth a 1,500-year-old underground church? If so, which post-Reformation church did it best resemble? Who had the best return-to-form? Was "faith alone" sitting on the sidelines, awaiting the limelight? Did an impossible "pre-Reformation Protestant" secretly meet with Luther to show him the real church and its Biblical beliefs? Since monumental reform commenced with a Catholic priest and his issues with the Church—and was further ignited by many other former Catholics—what could the reformers be returning to? And how would they know when they've reached satisfactory reform? Where is such a hidden church prophesied in the Bible? If most Christians were getting

11. Eyes Open

much of sacred Scripture and Tradition wrong from the first to the sixteenth century, what is left to believe?

In such context, Luther was the ultimate Biblical translator—the *Bishop of Tome*—with self-given authority to dilute the most significant message ever delivered to mankind: the terms of salvation.

. Why did the Catholic Church receive and recognize epistles that so "clearly" contradict her core teachings, especially in the universally accepted New Testament books? That seems rather self-defeating and one of the dumbest moves in history. At what point was canon deemed comprehensive? Is the Bible's table of contents inspired? Which translation is most inspired? Why isn't the Epistle of Barnabas included in canon? How about the First Epistle of Clement? Was it sacred Scripture or Tradition that led to the Bible in the first place? Did the Bible beget itself? If so, which version?

And who closed sacred canon? Before it was closed, under the new covenant, what did the Christian Church follow? Did early followers look over Paul's shoulder to ensure he didn't teach anything that wasn't reflected in his writing, lest he be guilty of spreading inconsistent Tradition? Or is there Scripture indicating that early Christians are to do their best until an official "Bible" is compiled and formalized, after which the REAL church can begin (assuming it follows the correct interpretation)?

Why was canon reopened? By what authority? Did the Gutenberg press usher in divine understanding—and developmental and copy editing—with first dibs going to Luther? And where does sola scriptura defend its own position in the Bible? Was that part taken out? Or is something so seismic simply self-evident? Therefore, is all scholarly exegesis definitive? When does something become scholarly? Who becomes his own Magisterium? His own Chair of Peter? Chair of Luther? Chair of Calvin? Chair of Joe? Chair of Jane?

What on earth is or is not infallible?

2 Timothy 3:16 doesn't read "All Scripture *alone*..." In fact, 2 Thessalonians 2:15 and 1 Timothy 3:15 refute such a notion.

Reject sacred Tradition by creating a new tradition? "All Scripture is inspired by God!"...as long as it aligns with _____'s perspective?

"It is not the gospel you believe, but yourself."

At what point would someone cross the line from sola scriptura to subtle generational, ever-modern translation—from sola scriptura to "Well, it's obviously implied" or "How can it mean anything else?" or the ever-subjective "If it doesn't contradict the Bible, it must be okay." According to who? How would personal struggles not foster new, ever-lenient theories backed by "iron-clad" verses? Or new translations to lessen human responsibility and further separate from Catholic, "obviously-heretical" teaching? Or to push agendas or alleviate some personal salvation burden? What about softer and softer directives and language? Mutable absolutes?

The path of least resistance.

The Bible is your oyster.

Who would stop anyone from inventing their own denomination? Is it not appealing, and perhaps even irresistible, to found a church and its doctrines in the name of correcting someone else's error or improving upon some "archaic" teaching? And if a standalone verse doesn't provide enough evidence, how about if jumbled with one or two more? There is an infinite number of "logical" combinations. Honestly, such errors can be created out of thin air, through any narrative's lens. From covenant to contract; from contract to conjured.

A self-interest necessity disguised as virtue.

Including Luther and Calvin, how could I trust anyone or anything that sprouted from such an erroneous institution? Since seventy percent of the Catholic Church's sacraments are

11. Eyes Open

dismissed by most Protestant churches, why wouldn't I proceed to question everything else and ditch Jesus Christ in the process? If the majority is wrong, which minority is right?

■ ■ ■

If Scripture is inspired, yet the understanding of such Scripture and resulting doctrines are wildly broad, then either:

A. no interpretations are inspired, or
B. only certain interpretations are inspired.

If A), the Bible and Christianity are pointless. If B), how would one determine who is right? Who would one trust? Who wins the crown of "inspired" interpreter? After all, at the top of every Christian denomination is a host of scholars, all making concrete claims and all believing the gravity of the Bible, that the "Scriptures obtain full authority among believers only when men regard them as having sprung from heaven, as if there the living words of God were heard" (to quote John Calvin).

As Reformed theologian Cornelius Van Til stated, "It is true that the best apologetics can be given only when the system of truth is well known. But it is also true that the system of truth is not well known except it be seen in its opposition to error."

But for anything to be deemed error, it must be measured against an absolute. If Holy Scripture is the ultimate system of truth, whose version of such truth is absolute? Without tradition, how would one know when a verse is finally, properly interpreted? Without tradition, does ancient writing perpetually and accurately capture a culture, a context, and a sentiment? If not, whose tradition and theology is best, and who or what is their source? After all, mankind can force the Bible to reflect—and submit to—any theology it desires.

Since errors are being reported as I write this very sentence, it seems reasonable to conclude we have never been closer to absolute truth. I'm sure we'll get there when enough scholars have had a chance to point out every inaccuracy in reason, soteriology, hermeneutics, exegesis, theology, and philosophy. Then, and only then, will we reach a "perfect" denomination of truth—one that every Christian can agree upon. Which, of course, would be followed by a newly discovered error. Another dog chasing its tail.

The further we get from the time of Christ and His direct commands to His apostles, the better we understand Him? The further we get from Christ, the wiser a select few become? A select few who would have to acknowledge their church's own tradition of determining what is acceptable interpretation and what is not, what is indisputable and what is merely good practice. A tradition with hierarchy, scandal, and sinful leaders and followers like every other establishment in human history.

From the onset of Reformation, it only took Andreas Karlstadt four years before he performed an abridged church service and seven years before he called Luther and his followers "new papists," as if to say, *The pioneers are not reformed enough! They should be aligned with my thoughts! And who are they to carry authority?!*

A year later, Huldrych Zwingli replaced Catholic Mass with his new Communion service.

That same year, Anabaptist Konrad Grebel rejected infant baptism and performed adult baptism.

In 1534, by declaring the Act of Supremacy, King Henry VIII became the head of a new church: the Church of England.

In 1541, only twenty-four years removed from Reformation, John Calvin introduced an entirely new church order, included in his *Ecclesiastical Ordinances*.

Confessions, creeds, or catechisms were then developed, all professing core tenets of each "true" church—each as binding as their founders decreed.

11. Eyes Open

From whistleblowers to lawmakers.

Since every new Christian denomination or movement claims to pinpoint some type of error and/or new revelation, "truth" and "proper authority" are aggressively multiplying. Maybe wildfires shouldn't be contained. Maybe heresy should be left to cytokinesis.

While continuing research, I found this question: *Who founded your church?*

Then I found a Martin Luther quote from his letter to the Christians of Antwerp. Even though the devil, not sola scriptura, is portrayed as the culprit, the letter gives pause to the danger of reform turned revolt—a revolt based and continued upon the most complex, confounding, and supernatural writing in human history. A revolt that has produced incessant, unmanageable correction.

Luther said:

> The devil...has devised a new [disturbance]; and begins to rage in his members, I mean in the ungodly, through whom he makes his way in all sorts of chimerical follies and extravagant doctrines. This won't have baptism, that denies the efficacy of the Lord's supper; a third, puts a world between this and the last judgment; others teach that Jesus Christ is not God; some say this, others that; and there are almost as many sects and beliefs as there are heads.
>
> I must cite one instance, by way of exemplification, for I have plenty to do with these sort of spirits. There is not one of them that does think himself more learned than Luther; they all try to win their spurs against me; and would to heaven that they were all such as they think themselves, and that I were nothing!

Whether Luther directly blamed Karlstadt, Zwingli, Grebel,

Calvin, or demonic spirits doesn't matter. Catastrophe was off to the races. With pride acting as an authority, the new, most dominant traditions marking the Reformation were:

1. by faith alone
2. by Scripture alone
3. by individual interpretation alone

Even if his initial focus was not to form a new church and doctrines, Luther remained akin to a fanatic prying doors open at an electronic store at 11:55 p.m. on Black Friday Eve, not foreseeing the tidal wave of zeal behind him. Once the 95-Theses crowbar was in place, crowds stampeded. Waldo, Wycliffe, and Hus were there in spirit, I'm sure. I can picture an employee getting trampled, shakily yelling, "One at a time, please!"

"Abuse of power!" and "Incorrect interpretation!" were now evermoving thresholds through which new and improved rebellion and sacrilege could pass—first by an inch, then a foot, then a yard, then a mile. Is the answer to travesties and missteps an exponential growth of the same?

An endless divorce: 9,500 theses and counting.

All is vanity and a striving after wind.

The Pieces Fit

Humbled by God, I reached an undeniable conclusion. In the process of reviewing all mainline Protestant denominations, I had considered joining either the Reformed church, the Baptist church, or the Churches of Christ, eventually realizing I would've kept bouncing from one to another until I found a porridge that was "just right" enough.

But, once again, I couldn't dodge the Holy Spirit. My vincible ignorance had nowhere to hide. Even as a practicing Protestant, what I had learned since my confession to Ashley, aligned

11. Eyes Open

perfectly with Catholic teaching. The most fitting paragraphs in the Catechism of the Catholic Church, nos. 2338, 2339, and 2342, state:

- "[The integrity of a chaste person] tolerates neither a double life nor duplicity in speech."
- "Chastity includes an *apprenticeship in self-mastery* which is a training in human freedom. The alternative is clear: either man governs his passions and finds peace, or he lets himself be dominated by them and becomes unhappy."
- "Self-mastery is a *long and exacting work*. One can never consider it acquired once and for all. It presupposes renewed effort at all stages of life."

On March 30, I returned to Mass. I made the sign of the cross, entered the nave, knelt in the third pew from the back, and proceeded to stare at the crucifix.

At peace.

I wept as I read the Nicene Creed: "...one, holy, catholic and apostolic Church..." A few weeks later, the Easter Sunday homily was about the Notre-Dame de Paris fire and Nat King Cole's *Mona Lisa*. The story of heartbreak and revival, grief and beauty, was among the most transcendent moments in my life. I sobbed, as did the presiding monsignor and many parishioners.

Leaving the Catholic Church had been like physically stepping over a creek; returning was like mentally crossing an ocean. I was home, but needed time to settle.

Now, when do I break the news to family and friends? For my parents, this would be a wonderful return. But for everyone else, would it seem like I was repurchasing that one-way ticket to hell?

One Flesh

At nineteen months into our journey, Ashley and I chatted at length about our disparate needs, and something new struck me: this intangible "thing" we'd been obsessing over was beyond *shelf life*, beyond hugging throughout the day, beyond affirmative words, beyond gestures of appreciation. These were, in fact, primers; the newfound truth was the paint.

From the time of confession, I had battled my flesh; discussed communication, love, intimacy, trust, faith, parenting, and religion for months with Ashley; and resisted some changes because *Haven't I done enough?* The whole time, I viewed any epiphany as a light bulb finally turned on in a dark room, only to uncover several more light bulbs. As I turned those on, several more appeared.

In this long series of light bulbs, I felt the one at hand had a sticker beneath it reading *homestretch*. As I reached to turn on this apparent penultimate bulb, I realized God is the greatest gift imaginable and nothing happens without His grace. In that moment, I knew I had never turned on a single bulb. It had always been Him. It was always my responsibility to act accordingly, regardless of my state of mind.

And what was the glaring challenge in front of me? To demonstrate the core of Holy Matrimony: unconditional love.

Because I enjoyed checking boxes, I often stoically "loved unconditionally." Again, my heart had no idea how to catch up to my head. Therefore, my facial expressions screamed insincerity for most of our relationship.

On this unique day, Ashley described a part of my heart she had only seen on occasion. I realized it could only be accessed when I was joyful, forgiving, thankful, and empty of my priorities. It was foreign and intimidating. Resentment and a look-what-I've-done attitude were much easier to accommodate.

11. Eyes Open

Ego-driven, victim-based action is simple. No thought is required. Conversely, love-driven self-denial requires not only intense focus, but a skyscraper of grace.

With Ashley and I clinging to a thread—as I felt we had been since the day we met—I comprehended what she was saying. It hit me on the outside and inside. I finally understood her words. It was the culmination of every epiphany I had received since first confessing on that horrid September night.

The key to her external vulnerability was my internal vulnerability. And the only way I could remain faithfully vulnerable was through long-term, unconditional sacrifice. Never again a façade. Gladly willing to be exposed, stay exposed, and place Ashley's needs above mine. The head for the sake of the body.

I sat back with a few simple thoughts: *I go first. He who loves his wife loves himself. I'd die to save her.*

■ ■ ■

Since childhood, Ashley had overwhelming convictions of what was right in marriage and family, but could never completely express them. They were always on the periphery, always just beyond reach. But by His grace, throughout our lengthy process, God confirmed what He had placed in her heart long ago—and she now saw these convictions through a new, distinguishable lens. A lens through which she had helped me become a better man, a better father, and a disciple. God had independently led us the entire time, orchestrating the impossible task of intersecting parallels.

And in this moment, I saw her for her, finally recognizing her God-given qualities. It all registered: her warmth, her compassion, her honesty, her faith, her discipline, her fidelity, her patience, and her care for me.

And the attributes I used to resent and criticize were

suddenly Ashley's most prized possessions. Much like the Catholic Church and what I viewed as its "laundry list of rules," what used to be viewed as high-maintenance was suddenly the biggest blessing imaginable.

Truly, law giving way to grace.

As a result, she had my full respect. It was genuine love. As I opened my innermost place—as deep as the dark recesses of my past—Ashley melted in my arms.

This began a process of morning and night prayers, always focused on the grace needed to see each other in the best light—to prepare ourselves for self-sacrifice. If not in the appropriate mindset, we had no business being intimate.

A few days later, a text read, *I love you more than you know*.

12. REFLECTION

Christ says "Give me All. I don't want so much of your time and so much of your money and so much of your work: I want You. I have not come to torment your natural self, but to kill it. No half-measures are any good. I don't want to cut off a branch here and a branch there, I want to have the whole tree down. I don't want to drill the tooth, or crown it, or stop it, but to have it out. Hand over the whole natural self, all the desires which you think innocent as well as the ones you think wicked—the whole outfit. I will give you a new self instead. In fact, I will give you Myself: my own will shall become yours."

—C. S. Lewis

It would be impossible to detail all the micro confessions that occurred over the two years. I'll never understand the minutiae God was drawing from me. He was sun rays striking a dusty room; my sins and temptations were thousands of motes.

Before navigating this process, I would've laughed at a man who believed this was God's handiwork. I probably would've joined shouts such as, "Come on, man! Porn is okay. So is divorce. Certain people aren't compatible. And masturbation? Dude, get real. It's a natural act. Everyone does it! And why disclose so much to your wife? Seems really stupid. That's what accountability partners and psychiatrists are for. You only did this because of guilt and neurosis! Your new favorite addictions are confession and insecurity. You said too much. It's your own striving after wind."

However, radical transparency and vulnerability—regardless of how futile and abnormal they may seem—can be used for good.

In regard to Christianity at large, as Martin Luther pointed out in his letter to fellow reformer Wolfgang Capito, "...everything should be unmasked, that there should be no tenderness, no excuses, no shutting one's eyes to anything, so that the truth may remain pure, visible, and open to the inspection of all."

Such a statement should include placing Luther himself under a microscope.

In regard to church regulations, in his *Commentary on the Epistle to the Galatians*, Luther described being tormented by the *law* of the Order of Saint Augustine:

> When I was a monk I tried ever so hard to live up to the strict rules of my order. I used to make a list of my sins, and I was always on the way to confession, and whatever penances were enjoined upon me I performed religiously. In spite of it all, my conscience was always in a fever of doubt. The more I sought to help my poor stricken conscience the worse it got. The more I paid attention to the regulations the more I transgressed them.

It is tempting to place blame on the religion in which one's idiosyncrasies and deficiencies are discovered or amplified. Religion is perhaps the most used—and convenient—scapegoat in

12. Reflection

history. In an effort to sidestep self-control, self-awareness, and responsibility, humanity tends to force causation where often—at best—correlation exists. However, this ignores nature, nurture, and one's mental state apart from said religion.

When reluctant to submit to God's will, accusing any *law* is a predictable tactic. Everything—aside from one's own subjectivity—becomes oppressive and erroneous.

If some students are mentally tormented while taking the notoriously demanding Master Sommelier Diploma Examination, should they request that the proctor recall and revise the test to alleviate their pain? Should they revise it themselves? Or should they humbly admit that personal struggles do not equate to something being wrong? Maybe it's better to learn from those who previously succeeded.

When forming any viewpoint, it's easy to investigate one side. To be intellectually honest, however, one must also consider opposing examples. For instance, Thomas of Villanova, who was an Augustinian monk around the same time as Luther, became a saint. The same Order, the same Rule, the same rigidity. By faith, one questioned the Biblical inclusion of the Book of James, calling it an "epistle of straw"; by following the Book of James, the other—by faith and works—sold his straw mattress to provide for the poor.

Maybe Luther's suggestion that "everything should be unmasked" complements Ephesians 5:11-17, indicating a dire need to purge, to return to nakedness, to risk humiliation in exchange for a renewed heart—for Catholic or Protestant, single or married. Perhaps transparency prevents an inch from becoming a mile, or from forming in the first place. Perhaps it boldly differentiates flesh and Spirit, and law and grace. Perhaps it cuts through vincible ignorance, fear of man, and cognitive dissonance. Perhaps it peers through the Reformation Wall, daring to investigate history, unaided by generational indictments against the Catholic Church.

Upon reflecting on it all, there was no other way for me. The feelings were too strong; the convictions were too severe.

The result: a born-and-raised Catholic operating within the confines of Protestantism. Akin to Luther and Johannes von Staupitz before the Reformation, I vomited on my "confessor," sparing nothing.

I didn't know what was transforming in me and my marriage until I was on the other side. I didn't even know what scrupulosity was until I was well into writing this book. Even the most terrible moments—those which seemed horribly deceptive—were making way for the profound. Thank God they didn't lead to a mental institution or the Church of Eddie, but to the Body of Christ.

Saint Alphonsus of Liguori writes,

> Many things appear to us to be misfortunes, but if we understood the end for which God sends them, we would see that they are graces. Contradictions, sickness, scruples, spiritual aridity and all the inner and outward torments are the chisel with which God carves his statues for Heaven.

God saw my countless errors and loved me enough to confront me, then took me on the most excruciating trek imaginable. It clearly took a high degree of change to help me understand the gravity of the His Word and His Church.

But what kept this painstaking process alive for so long? My stubbornness? Reluctance? Pride? Ignorance? For all I know, God wanted such an incomprehensible plan to play out and was cleaning house in a most unorthodox way—an approach that mere human logic and intellect cannot comprehend. I can't

12. Reflection

explain it, and I need to stop trying. Some mysteries are fine being left as is.

I'm sure many would shake their heads and laugh. Many theists would probably say the enemy tricked me, while many atheists—convinced that religion alone promotes guilt and shame—would say the two-year struggle was a result of imaginary laws.

One says, *If you can't prove it in the Bible, it's man-made.* Another says, *the Bible itself is man-made.* Another says, *until you can prove it with science, it's man-made.* Yet another says, *If you can't prove it with Hawking's theories, it's man-made.*

At such a point, I'd have to ask, *Who made that which is not man-made? And who made the one who made it?*

Then I'd consider what seem to be the most distilled paradoxes:

Either *nothing came from nothing, something came from nothing,* or *something always was.*

With these options, we all choose which people, mysteries, and presuppositions deserve our trust, each using a threshold for what is possible and impossible, natural and supernatural. Until we personally observe and study all phenomena on earth, we will forever rely on others' accounts and findings to shape our worldview. And regardless of where we land on the deity continuum—behind every answer, truth claim, confirmation bias, and burden of proof—one more humbling question will always remain.

Faith is inescapable.

Justified Sanctification

From the absurdity of my story, others may draw a conclusion: this arrangement must have been orchestrated by a spouse so insecure, proud, and unforgiving that she wanted to see her husband's pain forevermore.

Contrarily, it took a bride with such magnetic values and loyalty to stand with me as I learned how to die to self and give up myself for her. She was relentless in wanting to understand the puzzles of marriage and inherent challenges.

"Why is it this way?"

"Why are men designed like this? Why are women?"

"Why does culture portray women this way?"

"Why do women respond this way? Why do men?"

"Why are we so different?"

"Why are the emotional and physical so disjointed?"

Along the way, Ashley exhibited unconditional love. Truly unconditional. She stepped into the abyss of my soul and remained with me while being tormented herself the entire time. She previously only knew ten percent of me (truthfully, mostly the good parts). To love unconditionally in such circumstances was probably easy. But now, knowing every confessed sin represented a new "condition" to accept and forgive, it's clear God's grace supported her through it all. She said, "I have no idea how I stayed calm. It wasn't my doing. That wasn't me. That was God. It was His grace. If I had tried to handle all of your confessions and all of the pain and torment in my own strength, I would've completely lost it, and I'm sure our marriage would've been over."

Without Ashley and her sanctifying principles, I would have never dissected Saint Paul's instructions to the Ephesians. If she had been what the world says a woman should be, I would have never known chastity. I would have never picked up a cross. I would have never denied myself. I would have expected her to continually sacrifice, slowly dying inside, while I wallowed in filth.

As God revealed the hard truths of being a Christian man and husband, I always shared them with Ashley. It was either

12. Reflection

due to: simply feeling compelled; being a glutton for challenges (knowing many discoveries emphasized my leadership role and held me more accountable); or craving attention in the most perverse of ways. Think of it—I share something knowing it exposes more of my shortcomings, but at the same time I assume Ashley will be drawn to me for learning something of significance. It seems like the height of stupidity, but I'm sure my ego was yet again grasping at straws.

As C. S. Lewis states:

> On the other hand, you must realise from the outset that the goal towards which He is beginning to guide you is absolute perfection; and no power in the whole universe, except you yourself, can prevent Him from taking you to that goal. That is what you are in for. And it is very important to realise that. If we do not, then we are very likely to start pulling back and resisting Him after a certain point. I think that many of us, when Christ has enabled us to overcome one or two sins that were an obvious nuisance, are inclined to feel (though we do not put it into words) that we are now good enough. He has done all we wanted Him to do, and we should be obliged if He would now leave us alone. As we say "I never expected to be a saint, I only wanted to be a decent chap." And we imagine when we say this that we are being humble.

Much of the time I didn't know what was resistance, arrogance, or humility. I was simply surviving. Now I ask myself, *Was I supposed to make the opposite choice at times? If so, how many times? Would this have landed me in a better position, or would I have been diminishing the purpose of the journey? Did this need to play* out—*as strange and pointless as it seemed at times—in order to help others avoid similar struggles and patterns?*

Also, I wondered, *Whether I am enslaved or free, can I spin my wheels?* The answer is yes, of course I can. Even when out of Egypt, wandering the desert was enigmatic and often seemed meaningless. I'm not sure how much I got wrong in the process, but as I recited many times, "We know that in everything God works for good with those who love him, who are called according to his purpose" (Romans 8:28).

There is a reason Jesus said, "If any man would come after me, let him deny himself and take up his cross daily and follow me." My sinful nature often cried out, saying, *That's enough! I'm good.*

This was similar to playing video games as a child. When confronted with the most difficult levels, I dismissed bonuses, extra coins, tokens, and stars. I desired to beat the level, whether I was small or large, whether I had a boomerang or a slingshot, or whether I had one or many lives left. As I approached the final leg of each challenge, I was clammy and agitated, convinced I'd never play it again.

Realizing that the bare minimum is hardly an accomplishment, I eventually returned to each level, hoping to achieve excellence. It's the same in my spiritual life. My will loves to prematurely push through trials, only to have God ask me to retrace my steps and be willing to suffer while harvesting pearls of wisdom.

Through much ignorance, I've learned that if I decide *that's enough*, the risk of falling away from the Lord is real and nauseating. If I resolve to follow Christ and love my bride, it is a daily decision. The flesh operates in wind sprints, but the Spirit operates in marathons.

Admittedly, there were video games so challenging I never finished them, deciding instead to give up. I can picture Super Mario with his overconfident mustache smile, anticipating

12. Reflection

success before even starting, only to jump in lava within two seconds.

My life before God intervened.

Efficient Impatience

When I was called into the crucible of sanctification, I promptly merged onto an express lane. Then I chose a *basic* car wash in lieu of the *super-duper deluxe*. I wanted a simple external presoak, high-pressure wash, and spot-free rinse; God wanted that *plus* an internal and external undercarriage wash, wheel blaster, double presoak, tri-color foaming conditioner, clear coat protectant, tire dressing, removal of surface contaminants, removal of oxidation, carnauba wax, and contouring dry—with an exit sign reading: repeat as necessary for the rest of your life.

I've always wanted a quick fix. I still do. There's something so strong in my nature that desires to run from prolonged, steady, heart-challenging discipline. I would have conveniently branded this dysfunction as a desire for efficiency. Whatever I wanted, I wanted instantly. In any setting, patience was torture.

For example, at the grocery store, when trying to choose the right checkout line, in a matter of ten seconds, I was programmed to evaluate the ages of the shoppers (predicting whether or not they'd be paying with a check), the number of items in each cart, the propensity of each shopper to chat with the clerk, and the aptitude of each shopper in the self-checkout line. I then made my decision.

However—no matter how hard I tried—I'd end up in one of the slowest lines.

My life every time I took the wheel.

Track & Yield

Anytime I tire from running on God's chosen path—failing to remain in tight communion with Him—mental harassment intensifies. Similar to Saint Paul's thorn in the flesh, when this "thing" of the enemy pesters me, God's grace is beside me, inspiring me to return to the track and endure in sanctification.

Chasing His will is a challenge that keeps my pride in check and my walk focused. A test that reminds me that law and grace, duty and privilege, can easily become unbalanced and distorted if I creep towards victimhood, cynicism, or idleness.

Regardless of what has been accomplished through obedience and repentance, there is an ever-present mystery about my walk. Firm reliance and faint anxiety dance in the background, drawing me back to God and the race of perseverance. It is neither condemnation nor comfort. It is where joy and sorrow alternate; where pride tries to grip me, yet humility continues to fight; where love gains ground but often falls short; and where I'm shown the depth of my sins and my need for ongoing correction. It lands squarely at the intersection of: "...for in this hope we were saved"; "...work out your salvation with fear and trembling"; and "...he who endures to the end will be saved."

At this confluence, faith, hope, and charity advance.

Anytime this "thing" of the enemy departs, a baton is left in its place—and "so great a cloud of witnesses" shout with encouragement as I rejoin the field of marathoners.

Insanity Now, Serenity Later

Fearing how others would respond to my recent leg of the race, I awkwardly traversed much of God's track without counsel. I assumed I'd be mocked and told that God wouldn't direct such a tragedy, or, simply, "Abandon ship!" Certainly, no one had been

12. Reflection

called to confess so many sins—to his wife! Certainly, no one had experienced such confusion. Certainly, no one ceaselessly desired to give up, only to find that defeat was the worst possible option. I know these were lies, but it sure felt rewarding to validate them.

Well over a hundred times, I thought the pilgrimage was complete, only to find an additional installment of burning refinement and humiliation. If plotted on a chart with a random, one-month duration selected, the journey would appear pointless and the future hopeless. But, if zoomed out with an expanded duration, significant growth would be evident. It's through a long-term view that I see the dividends of our investment.

If I had decided to pursue purity without God's involvement, I would have stopped the progress as I reached my own comfort level—which, at best, would've been defined by pop-culture-Christianity. Ultimately, with everything I had observed and learned, it boiled down to a number of questions:

- Does moral objectivity exist?
    - If so, do I want to be corrected in order to align with such truth?
    - If not, is it because I desire to be my own authority?
- Do I believe in God?
    - If so, is Jesus Christ also God?
    - If so, did Jesus Christ institute a Church?
    - If so, does the Church remain?
    - If so, which one?
- Apart from submission to God and His Church, how would I even know sanctification?

With the answers, He continues to take me beyond anything I thought normal, acceptable, or possible.

■ ■ ■

In the mire of it all, considering how backward everything appeared, I understandably felt judged and critiqued by many of those who only knew about my unemployment. Whenever I zealously shared additional portions of our struggle, I felt even less believable. I pictured people blaming my irrational decisions on head trauma caused by that car at Fresno State.

I'd love to use that as an excuse for everything I can't explain, but that wouldn't be right. The convenient answer to any radical faith journey is to claim it's purely a mind game. Heck, if a large part of this mess wasn't in our rearview mirror, I would likely think the same thing about anyone with similar experiences. But, although outwardly illogical, I know it was real because God annihilated many spirit, soul, and body dysfunctions.

Undeniably, however, more remain.

Still Maturing

When our house sold, I was convinced we had budgeted correctly to cover us until our certificate-of-deposit maturation date, but, sadly, we stumbled financially. We overspent by purchasing some furniture, kitchen items, and other goods we sought for comfort or convenience. We did the same with food.

Our excuses were locked and loaded.

- "Let's just get takeout. I don't have the energy to cook for the kids."
- "Oh, who cares right now. We're trying to survive!"
- "We'll worry about that later."
- "It's okay. It's not like we eat like this all the time."
- "Let's take the kids to get ice cream and Starbucks."

I often internally reasoned, *It's Friday!* as if the day of the week

12. Reflection

magically supplied us with more frivolous money. These were immature reactions to the sewage we were plodding through—a reward of some sort.

In early May 2019, just like the year before when we were in escrow, we were about to run out of money, and our CD wasn't set to mature until the end of June. Back to the garage we went, looking for anything we missed. We also sold some of our new furniture. Once those options were exhausted, we liquidated the rest of our 401(k).

Meanwhile, while my work hours were topping at ten a week, a few wine recruiters emailed, wanting me to consider various roles. Clearly another test. I declined, saying I was happy in healthcare. I imagined the shouts: "You're such an idiot!"

Dave Ramsey would not have advocated selling our house, cracking—then frying—our nest egg, and failing to adhere to a strict financial plan. However, budgeting mistakes aside, I knew we were called to something outrageous.

Something well beyond bucking convention.

Something screaming madness to most.

But on we trudged.

■ ■ ■

On a Tuesday evening, Ashley's mom and grandparents came over for dinner. Having just sold an expensive table for twelve, we crowded around our newest fixture: a card table that sat four. However, all eight of us squeezed in, said a prayer, and began to eat.

Before taking a bite, Arlo turned to his great grandfather and asked, "Where do you find a dog with no legs?"

With a smirk, he replied, "I don't know...."

"Where you left him."

Father's Day

On the evening of June 7, Ashley approached me with a confusing grin as she entered our bedroom.

"What's going on?" I asked.

"I hate having to wait to give gifts," she responded.

"What gift?"

"It's for Father's Day. I don't want to wait another week."

With strong anticipation, I said, "Go ahead if you think it's best." *Who am I to argue?*

She headed for the far end of the room and told me to close my eyes. A few seconds later, she led me forward about five steps, all to keep me guessing.

"Ready?" she asked.

"Sure," I said, as I opened my eyes.

Baby #4. Due February 14, 2020.

To Whom Shall We Go?

On August 19, I went to my first Catholic confession in over fifteen years. Unknowingly, I had been preparing for such a moment for two years. Fittingly, I requested to meet face-to-face with my parish priest.

The following day, after having been wed at a winery just shy of ten years earlier, our marriage was convalidated by the Catholic Church. At the same private ceremony, Arlo, Eviana, and Zion were baptized. Ashley, still shell-shocked from our voyage, was in a daze. As beautiful as ever, she stood by my side, probably wondering, *HOW?*

In a matter of six months, she had absorbed waves of theology; studied, then resisted, then studied some more; watched me fumble through apologetics; wrestled with the fact that the majority of her internal convictions aligned with Catholic teaching;

12. Reflection

and asked dozens of macro questions, as well as brilliant micro questions—several of which we wouldn't find answers to. Regardless, she resolved to join the Church and raise the children Catholic even though, like me, she couldn't comprehend many mysteries of the faith. An exacting process, starting with a five-hundred-year quantum leap.

On Saturday evening, August 24, five months after my initial return, I entered the church doors with new awe. As I made the sign of the cross, I entered the nave, knelt in the third pew from the front, and prepared to receive the Holy Eucharist for the first time in well over a decade. By God's grace, I was in His presence, once again at peace.

The following week—on some random day, at some random time, in some random room—Ashley turned to me, saying, "You claimed that God confronted you two years ago. I've watched Him work on you this whole time. I've actually seen the fruit myself. You're a completely different man. And you claimed God did it again and led you to Catholicism. If I hadn't seen you change so dramatically, I never would've taken you seriously. I never would've been willing to even consider Catholicism. But because I've watched you obey God every single time—even when it looked absolutely insane—I trust you. Your obedience is the only reason I'm here."

Shortly thereafter, the agonizing, oppressive, harassing presence known as scrupulosity died. With a sense of relief beyond understanding, I wanted to cry, but I remained in shock and nothing came out.

Disorder Cannot Be Outrun

If God had not confronted me, Ashley and I would be destined for divorce, yet still playing dress-up as a normal, healthy couple with a bright future. Our marriage, after nine, fourteen, twenty-seven, or even thirty-eight years, was sure to detonate. Both of us would have continued dying inside, suffering from each other's wounds. Through sheer determination, stubbornness, and stoicism, we would have reached a threshold, then our dam would've burst.

But we now know each other better than anyone else possibly could. All our strengths, motives, uncertainties, shortcomings, talents, doubts, proclivities, dreams, and trials; whether good or bad, we know each other.

Ashley and I walked through our perception of hell and have resolved to stay focused on the operative word: *through*. If we had left each other, new and improved rebellion would await us in subsequent marriages or relationships; if we had complacently stayed together, we would have persisted in bondage to an array of coping sins.

I bet leaving each other in the midst of disgrace would have pridefully forced us to reason: *Yes, of course the grass is greener! It has to be. It has to.* However, a new relationship was not the answer to our story's dilemma. We could not improve upon or replicate our covenant by replacing it with a contract. We were meant to be reconciled despite travesties and missteps. We just needed secrets to be known, weaknesses and intentions to be exposed, and hearts to be revealed and converted—with God at the center. Without Him, we fail.

I think back to Genesis 2:16-17, realizing the verses exemplify the distinction between being with God and apart from God. When I was far from Him, I only saw, "*...but* of the tree of the knowledge of good and evil *you shall not eat...*" (emphasis added). But when I drew close, my focus became, "You may *freely eat* of every tree of the garden..." (emphasis added). The difference between the two is paramount. One paints a picture of cynicism and tyranny; the other discipline, love, and grace. Until this journey, I could not decipher the latter. I only saw

12. Reflection

what I was not supposed to do; I saw a catalog of rules, not a guiding light of decrees.

Pornography, masturbation, and alcohol consumption all ceased the day I confessed to Ashley, without exception. And my dreams no longer haunt me.

Granted, in our journey to a secure, undefiled, thriving marriage, we occasionally find residual triggers, insecurity, and confusion. However, these byproducts are mere jabs in light of the haymakers we endured in the early stages.

As we wade through remaining dysfunctions (as God reveals them), we still battle health and finances, but our faith and marriage have never been stronger. Despite many epiphanies, we still wrestle with the delicate, complicated convergence of love, respect, and intimacy. Another exacting process.

Although its meaning has dramatically changed, I still "confess" to my grafted best friend and accountability partner. Instead of shameful sins or scrupulous, trivial errors, I simply share deep thoughts with my better half—and she joyfully reciprocates.

God did it all. As Ashley and I partnered with Him, He refused to let go of our hands. Because of Him, we are new creations. Through the Church's sacraments, we are determined to continually allow God to cleanse us and our marriage. Better now than later.

Ashley, my beauty. Devoted wife and mother of my children. The relentless one. The one who follows me and fights for us. 'Til death.

Our gift from God: His divine interventions. †

No one knows what he himself is made of, except his own spirit within him, yet there is still some part of him which remains hidden even from his own spirit; but you, Lord, know everything about a human being because you have made him[...]Let me, then, confess what I know about myself, and confess too what I do not know, because what I know of myself I know only because you shed light on me, and what I do not know I shall remain ignorant about until my darkness becomes like bright noon before your face.

—Saint Augustine, *Confessions*

CHRONOLOGY

2007

November: Eddie and Ashley meet at Starbucks.

2009

September: Eddie and Ashley get married.

2012

June: Ashley tells GP she's pregnant with Arlo.

2016

February: Eddie and Ashley's second child, Eviana, is born.

August: Ashley's receives rheumatoid arthritis and lupus diagnoses.

November: Eddie receives first conviction to get baptized as an adult.

2017

February: Eddie gets baptized.

April & May: Eddie and Ashley begin the AIP diet.

July: Eddie loses his wine job.

September: Eddie is confronted by God. He begins confessing to Ashley.

November: Eddie and Ashley attend a marriage retreat.

2018

February: Ashley tells Eddie she's pregnant with their third child.

April: Eddie and Ashley list their house in Napa.

June: Escrow closes. Eddie and Ashley move to Vacaville.

October: Eddie and Ashley's third child, Zion, is born.

December: Eddie lands a healthcare admin job and begins writing *Confession All*.

2019

February: Eddie is confronted by God again. This time about Catholicism.

March: Eddie attends his first Holy Mass in over ten years.

June: Ashley begins taking online RCIA (Rite of Christian Initiation of Adults) classes. Ashley tells Eddie she's pregnant with their fourth child.

August: Eddie and Ashley's marriage is convalidated by the Catholic Church. Arlo, Eviana, and Zion are baptized.

SOURCES

Adam, Peter. *Hearing Gods Words: Exploring Biblical Spirituality*. Apollos, 2005.
Alighieri, Dante. *The Divine Comedy of Dante Alighieri*. Oxford University Press, 2003.
Augustine, and Henry Chadwick. *Confessions*. Oxford University Press, 2008.
Augustine. *Sermons: inter A.D. 391-430*.
Bernard, et al. *Bernard of Clairvaux: Selected Works*. HarperSanFrancisco, 2005.
Bouwsma, William J. "John Calvin." *Encyclopedia Britannica*, Encyclopedia Britannica, Inc., 4 Feb. 2020, www.britannica.com/biography/John-Calvin.
Bromiley, Geoffrey W. "Huldrych Zwingli." *Encyclopedia Britannica*, Encyclopedia Britannica, Inc., 1 Jan. 2020, www.britannica.com/biography/Huldrych-Zwingli.
Catechism of the Catholic Church. Libreria Editrice Vaticana, 2019.
Chadwick, Owen. *John Cassian: A Study in Primitive Monasticism*. 1968.
Edwards, Mark U., Jr. Printing, Propaganda, and Martin Luther. Berkeley: University of California Press, 1994. bit.ly/2TAfexu
"EWTN Live (Fr. Mitch Pacwa & Dr. Scott Hahn)." 7 Nov. 2018.
Hillerbrand, Hans J. "Martin Luther." *Encyclopedia Britannica*, Encyclopedia Britannica, Inc., 14 Feb. 2020, www.britannica.com/biography/Martin-Luther.
Holy Bible: New International Version. Zondervan, 2005.
Ignatius, and Thomas Corbishley. *The Spiritual Exercises of Saint Ignatius of Loyola*. Newton Abbot, 2011.
Jones, Frederick M. *Alphonsus De Liguori: Saint of Bourbon Naples, 1696-1787, Founder of the Redemptorists*. Liguori, 1999.
Lewis, C. S. *Mere Christianity*. HarperCollins Publishers, 2017.
Lucado, Max, and Sergio Martinez. *You Are Mine*. Christian Art, 2006.
Luther, Martin, and Theodore Grebner. *Commentary on the Epistle to the Galatians*. Concordia Seminary, 2015.
Merton, Thomas. *Thoughts in Solitude*. Farrar, Straus, Giroux, 2000.
Metaxas, Eric. *Martin Luther: the Man Who Rediscovered God and Changed the World*. Penguin Books, 2018.

Michelet, Jules. *The Life of Martin Luther: Gathered from His Own Writings*. University of Michigan, 2007.

Morrill, John S., and Geoffrey R. Elton. "Henry VIII." *Encyclopedia Britannica*, Encyclopedia Britannica, Inc., 24 Jan. 2020, www.britannica.com/biography/Henry-VIII-king-of-England.

"One Layman's Guide to Spiritual Survival." *Google Books*, Google, bit.ly/2wt7sxw.

Seuss. *The Sneetches and Other Stories*. Random House, 1989.

"How to Psychoanalyze Yourself." *Life Is Worth Living*, ABC, 1957.

"The Double." *Ultraman Story: Vito Bialla : Ultraman World Championships*, ultramanlive.com/history/contestants-stories/ultraman-story-vito-bialla/.

The Editors of Encyclopedia Britannica. "Konrad Grebel." *Encyclopedia Britannica*, Encyclopedia Britannica, Inc., 1 Jan. 2020, www.britannica.com/biography/Konrad-Grebel.

The Ignatius Catholic Study Bible, Revised Standard Version. 2nd ed., Ignatius Press, 2010.

Til, Cornelius Van. *The Defense of the Faith: an Introduction to Systematic Theology*. Presbyterian and Reformed Pub. Co., 1974.

Made in the USA
Las Vegas, NV
20 July 2025